Perspective on Man

PERSPECTIVE ON MAN

Literature and the Christian Tradition

BY ROLAND MUSHAT FRYE

THE WESTMINSTER PRESS · *Philadelphia*

Library of Congress Catalog Card No. 61–10828

PRINTED IN THE UNITED STATES OF AMERICA

To
the memory of my Father
who in an active life exemplified
the love of learning, of literature, and of the
Christian faith

17420

Contents

ACKNOWLEDGMENTS

It is a pleasure to acknowledge my indebtedness to the faculty and administration of the Princeton Theological Seminary for the invitation to deliver the L. P. Stone Lectures for 1959, which form the basis of this little book. For their helpfulness and support I owe a great debt to many friends and former professors of mine on the faculties both of Princeton Seminary and of Princeton University, and especially in connection with these lectures to Dr. Emile Cailliet and to Dr. John Alexander Mackay. Among my colleagues at Emory University, Ward Pafford and Jack Boozer were generous in their criticism and suggestions, as was my friend Shirley Guthrie, of the Columbia Theological Seminary faculty. It is a pleasure, too, to acknowledge the unfailing helpfulness and efficiency of Miss Charlotte Williams, who carried this manuscript through its various stages and assisted in innumerable other ways.

I also wish to acknowledge my gratitude to the following publishers and copyright holders who have graciously allowed me to quote from creative writings over which they exercise control: E. P. Dutton & Co., Inc., for the Wicksteed and Oelsner edition of Dante's *Divine Comedy;* for numerous quotations from T. S. Eliot's *The Cocktail Party,* copyright 1950, *The Complete Poems and Plays,* copyright 1952, and *Murder in the Cathedral,* copyright 1935, all by permission of Harcourt, Brace and Company, Inc., and also for quotations from *The Antigone of Sophocles: An English Version* by Dudley Fitts and Robert Fitzgerald, copyright 1939, by Harcourt, Brace and Company, Inc.; Harper & Brothers for Aldous Huxley's *Brave New World* and *Brave New World Revisited;* Prof. Gilbert Highet and Book-of-the-Month Club for "Mass Culture"; Holt, Rinehart and Winston, Inc., for Robert Frost's "The Figure a Poem Makes" from *Complete Poems* and for excerpt from "To a Contemporary Bunkshooter" from *Chicago Poems,* by Carl Sandburg, copyright 1916 by Henry Holt & Co., Inc., and copyright 1944 by Carl Sandburg; Little, Brown & Co. for Peter de Vries' *The Mackerel Plaza* and *The Tunnel of Love* and for J. D. Salinger's *The Catcher in the Rye;* Longmans,

Green & Co., Inc. for Geddes MacGregor's *From a Christian Ghetto;* The Macmillan Company for W. B. Yeats' translation of Sophocles' *King Oedipus* and C. S. Lewis' *The Abolition of Man;* New Directions for permission to reprint excerpts from *Cat on a Hot Tin Roof,* copyright 1955 by Tennessee Williams; W. W. Norton & Company, Inc., for Edith Hamilton's translation of Aeschylus' *Prometheus Bound* and for her *The Greek Way to Western Civilization* and *The Roman Way;* Oxford University Press and Christopher Fry for Christopher Fry's *The Lady's Not for Burning, A Sleep of Prisoners,* and *Thor, With Angels,* and for Charles W. Kennedy's translation *Early English Christian Poetry;* Penguin Books, Ltd., for E. F. Watling's translation of *The Theban Plays* of Sophocles; Princeton University Press for Charles W. Kennedy's translation *Old English Elegies;* Random House, Inc., for Eugene O'Neill's *The Hairy Ape,* copyrighted 1922 and renewed 1949 by Eugene O'Neill, from the Random House edition of *Nine Plays,* by Eugene O'Neill; Charles Scribner's Sons for passages reprinted with the permission of Charles Scribner's Sons from *Abe Lincoln in Illinois,* by Robert Emmet Sherwood, copyright 1939 Robert Emmet Sherwood; Sheed & Ward, Ltd., for Henry N. Wells' edition of *Piers Plowman;* the Society of Authors and Mrs. Cicely Binyon for Laurence Binyon's translation of Dante's *Divine Comedy;* the Society of Authors and the Public Trustee for George Bernard Shaw's *Back to Methuselah, Major Barbara,* and *Saint Joan;* the University of Chicago Press for Gilbert Murray's *Literature of Ancient Greece; World Theatre* and l'Institut International du Théâtre for Christopher Fry's "Why Verse?" Full references to each one of these works are provided both in the Notes and in the Bibliography. In addition to these creative works or translations of creative works for which specific acknowledgments are made here and elsewhere, I wish to express my thanks to the scholars whose works I have cited in the following pages. Within the fraternity of learning, my debt to these and to others is great indeed.

Then there is my son, who has helped me by being patient and understanding, and my wife, whose suggestions, criticisms, and encouragement have been invaluable.

ROLAND MUSHAT FRYE

Department of English
Emory University

Introduction

INTRODUCTION

Some four and a quarter centuries ago, Martin Luther wrote a letter in which he made, with brevity and force, a profoundly significant analysis of the relationship between Christianity and literary culture. "I am persuaded," Luther wrote, "that without knowledge of literature pure theology cannot at all endure, just as heretofore, when letters have declined and lain prostrate, theology, too, has wretchedly fallen and lain prostrate; nay, I see that there has never been a great revelation of the Word of God unless He has first prepared the way by the rise and prosperity of languages and letters, as though they were John the Baptists. . . . Certainly it is my desire that there shall be as many poets and rhetoricians as possible, because I see that by these studies, as by no other means, people are wonderfully fitted for the grasping of sacred truth and for handling it skillfully and happily. . . . Therefore I beg of you that at my request (if that has any weight) you will urge your young people to be diligent in the study of poetry and rhetoric."[1] Luther's judgment here is immensely suggestive for the serious study of literature and of theology, for it indicates the existence of important relationships which are too often ignored. If it is true, as Luther thought, that "without knowledge of literature pure theology cannot at all endure," then the relationships between literature and Christian theology assume very great importance.

The general perspective of Martin Luther's statement and of this book is the perspective of Christian humanism. Historians of culture, and especially perhaps historians of literature, use the term "Christian humanism" to describe a consciously Christian approach to literature, philosophy, and other humanistic disciplines. The depth, strength, and diver-

13

sity of the tradition of Christian humanism may best be defined by recalling that it includes Augustine, Dante, Erasmus, Zwingli, Melanchthon, Calvin, Sir Philip Sidney, John Milton, and Dr. Samuel Johnson, to name only a few. To note that these men are Christian humanists is not to imply that they represent a single philosophical position, for Christian humanism is not to be defined simply as a philosophy—and certainly not as the philosophy of humanism—but rather as a disciplined and dedicated concern for the relations between traditional Christianity and humane culture.

The relationship between Christianity and literature has traditionally been a close one, and it has never been closer than during the early centuries of Protestantism. In more recent generations, however, Protestants have too often tended to minimize connections which the early Reformers, and later the English Puritans, regarded as extremely important, if not indeed essential. My primary purpose here is to outline in broad terms and for our own time the nature of the relationships between the best of man's literature and the Christian faith, and it is to this purpose that the five chapters of this book will be devoted. The early Protestant attitudes toward literature are so significant, however, that I have treated them at considerable length in an appendix, which will clearly demonstrate the importance which representative Protestants attached to the subject in the sixteenth, seventeenth, and eighteenth centuries.

The primary concern of this book remains to re-establish the claims of Christian humanism in our time. The relations between Christianity and literature can certainly not be exhausted in the course of one small book, but it will be possible to show the continuing validity and relevance of Christian humanism by discussing within a Christian perspective the human experience and insight which is preserved in great literary works. In this effort, we will draw upon the literature of Asia as well as of Greece and Rome, and the non-Christian literature of the West as well as the great masterpieces of Christian imagination.

Literature may be related to the Christian faith in three ways: first, as literary method in the use of symbol, metaphor, and story is applicable to the understanding of Biblical truth; second, as literature treats, in basic and universal terms, both the affirmations and the problems of human existence with which theology must come to grips; and last, as specific writers express their visions of life in terms of a Christian frame of reference. These three approaches to our subject will form the three sections into which this book is divided, and although these three approaches provide the means for a full view of the subject, our analyses under each of the three sections will be representative rather than exhaustive.

The first chapter will discuss the relevance of literary method to theological understanding, taking up the manner in which awareness of the distinctive literary approaches to truth may serve Christian theology. We will consider here the characteristic principles which operate in the serious literary treatment of history, as well as the manner in which truth is conveyed through literary fictions, symbols, and metaphors. The literary creation of beauty might well have been placed here, as literature operates creatively through beauty, but I have postponed the consideration of beauty until the second chapter. My concern with literary method in the opening chapter is with its relevance to theology, for which beauty is not necessary although it is surely desirable.

A major contribution of literary understanding to theology comes in the development of a power of thought which goes beyond the surface, which sees through the symbol to the larger referent. A mechanical literalizing and a philosophical demythologizing are two of the gravest dangers to which Scriptural analysis may succumb. That early Reformation theologians avoided these extremes is due in no small measure to humanistic taste and influence.

The explication of Scripture is, after all, a *literary* problem, and when the early Reformers called for a return to the level of the *litera* they were not calling for a mechanical concentration upon what modern fundamentalism means by literalism. They were, rather, calling for a concern with the *literary* meaning of the text considered by the best methods available to them as Christian humanists. Thus they would rescue Scripture from the fantastic embellishments of scholastic ingenuity. They would rescue it not only in terms of the "proper" meaning of simple statement but also by organic reference to metaphoric and to compound or composite meanings—in terms of a fully literary exegesis, in the attempt to recover the meaning of the text itself. Thus, according to Luther, "without knowledge of literature pure theology cannot at all endure." The first section of the book will be concerned, then, with the manner in which literary method contributes to theological understanding.

The second section of the book, consisting of Chapters Two and Three, will consider certain representative and significant affirmations and problems in terms of which literature analyzes human life. Literature may analyze and support the greatness of man, as we shall see in the second chapter, and yet it also deals with the tragic limits of human endeavor and achievement, as we shall see in Chapter Three. In these chapters we will be concerned with the basically human, with affirmations and questionings which seem to be universally relevant to the situations of men and to which Christianity as a universal religion must speak. Literature is probably the most faithful mirror of human existence which man can create, and whereas the third and final section of this book will treat distinctively Christian responses to the greatness and misery of man as mirrored in literature, the second section is concerned with what man has best said about himself and his world. Prior to the coming of God's response to man's situation, the most significant thing which man can do is to analyze himself and his place in the world, and here the religious significance of his literature may be found even more in the questions raised than in the affirmations given, though both are important.

Of course questions are neither raised, nor responded to, in literature as they are in Aquinas' *Summa,* for example, for in literature the problems are more fully involved in the great wholeness of human existence. Problems are explored and exposed in a context of occurrences and of encounter rather than of abstraction and of logic. The clash of discordant ethics, the tensions of changing values, the search for some valid personal identity in a world of conflicting natures (as in *King Lear*); the problem of choice between goods and evils, the conflicts within the self, the ultimate despair of ethics (as in *Oedipus*); the search for a pleasure which is beyond the reach of pain and of duty, the mysterious weakness of the great, and the paradox of hedonism (as in *Antony and Cleopatra*)—all of these and other galaxies of problems are analyzed in the unabstracted context of the imitation of life which is literary art. Basic problems are explored, exhibited, clarified, though not necessarily solved. Thus it is that an imaginative and perceptive "heathen" work may be of far more religious value in terms of the second type of relationship between theology and literature than an unimaginative and sterile parroting of orthodox clichés under a literary disguise.

In the second section, then, we will treat successively the literary nurturing of man's greatness and the literary questionings of that greatness. In explicit terms, we will treat in Chapter Two the purposes of humane literature as these have been expressed by its masters and the manner in which it furnishes insight into human life and increases the value of that life by the nurture of beauty, of understanding, and of compassion. Literature thus achieves what Shelley described as arranging the various elements of experience "according to a certain rhythm and order which may be called the beautiful and the good," so that the poet serves as one of "the unacknowledged legislators of the world."[2] In this way, literature (regardless of whether or not it is Christian) both treats and enhances the greatness of man, as we will see by the example of works both ancient and modern. In Chapter Three we will notice how great literature (regardless, again, of whether it is Christian) serves man by bringing to light the ultimate dilemmas of the human soul, posing the universal problems of human existence so as to expose not only man's triumph and greatness, but also his limits, his failure, and his need. Here we will examine some of the more significant literary treatments of the representatively human problems of death, of identity, and of guilt.

The first three chapters will thus be seen to deal with certain universals of human existence, as we draw from a rather wide range of literature both Christian and non-Christian. Following the treatment of the tragic limits of man's existence, the two final chapters, which make up the third section of the book, will be primarily concerned with the distinctively Christian orientations toward life which are to be found in explicitly Christian literature. By this term I do not mean the strained efforts to reinforce pious platitudes by fiction and poetry, or the soap-opera renditions of a popular moralism. I refer to the great mainstream which includes Dante, Langland, Milton, Bunyan, and, in our own time, T. S. Eliot and Christopher Fry.

Writers such as these not only clarify the greatness and the limits of man, and direct us in the specifically literary approach to knowledge, but also mediate the Christian revelation to us. This mediation may vary in extent (more will be contained in Milton's *Paradise Lost* than in his Sonnet XIX on his blindness) and in intensity (a more vital awareness of God may be conveyed to a particular reader through the sonnet than through the epic, for example). But in whatever extent or intensity, Christian revelation is mediated through such distinctively Christian works.

The works of creative writing are obviously different from the work of theologies statementally defined. For one thing, they bring the reader into more direct encounter with persons through events. Structured as they are, Dante's works, or Bunyan's, or Milton's, move the readers to be not merely thinkers about, but at least during the time of literary exposure, to be thinking and feeling participants in the Christian drama. Such is the nature of the literary mode. The essential drama is the same in each case—Jesus Christ as the supreme revelation remains central and originative—but the relations are reordered in terms of the illumination of the creative artist. The reader is then caught up in the events, in the encounter with persons and occurrences, and so is existentially confronted with the Supreme Encounter and with the ways of life which issue from it. Whether this existential encounter is accepted is another question, but it is at least forcefully presented through the works of Christian imagination.

The fourth chapter will discuss the manner in which the three crucial questions of death, identity, and guilt are met in the literary masterpieces of a distinctively Christian imagination. The meeting of these problems by Christian faith in such a manner that man is rescued from sin and death and established in a new identity will be discussed in terms of the literary analyses of redemption. In the fifth and final chapter we will turn to the sequel of that redemption as it is expressed in various accounts of the Christian battles in the

Holy War and of the Christian pilgrimage from the Dark Wood of Error to the City of God.

This, then, is the general structure which will be followed, but at the base of everything which is said here is the clear assumption which every Christian humanist will hold, and which cannot be better expressed than in the words used by Prof. Charles G. Osgood in his brilliant Stone Lectures for 1940: "Secular literature cannot equal Holy Writ in power or authority or efficacy as a means of grace. Yet it may illustrate, reinforce, verify, and illuminate Holy Writ. . . . It may serve us as the sycamore tree served Zacchaeus, to gain a clearer sight of the Incarnate Truth."[3]

PART I

*Literary Understanding
and Biblical Truth*

Chapter One

THE LETTER AND THE SPIRIT

That literature is engaged in the pursuit of truth as well as the pursuit of beauty has been a perennial understanding both of serious literary artists and of serious literary critics. And those who have most insisted upon the truth-bearing function of literature have been equally insistent that the manner in which literature approaches truth is different from the manner in which other disciplines approach truth. Literary truth is thus not proverbial truth, nor is it ethical precept, nor scientific accuracy, nor historical verisimilitude, nor philosophic logic. It is concerned neither with the development of abstract principles nor with the accumulation of accurate observations, but rather with the creation of living situations in which the reader is invited to become involved. Thus, according to the Renaissance beau ideal Sir Philip Sidney, Alexander the Great found his own tutor Aristotle to be in some ways less instructive than the long-dead poet Homer, for "he received more bravery of mind by the pattern of Achilles, than by hearing the definition of fortitude."[1] In making a similar comparison between literature and philosophy, the great Italian writer Boccaccio declared that while the philosopher approached truth by means of syllogistic logic, the poet approached truth by means of exquisitely wrought fictions.[2] And Shelley declared it "presumptuous" to

23

assume that the only methods of mental operation are syllogistic, "when mental effects are experienced unsusceptible
of being referred to them."[3]

Now the relevance of these distinctive literary approaches
to truth for the understanding of Christian Scripture is im-
mense, and it is here that the methods of literary analysis are
particularly relevant to theological endeavor. For purposes of
convenience, I wish to approach these relevant methods in
this chapter under two general headings: first, the literary
approach to truth through the dramatic presentation of history, and then the literary approach to truth through non-
historical or fictional categories.

I. *Dramatic and Biblical History*

Christianity is inextricably involved in history by its understanding of man's relation to God in the past, in the
present, and in the future. It is basically geared to acts, events,
and meanings in history rather than to the patent and recur-
ring cycles of nature or to some hypothetical and idealized
timeless truths. Nature religions, expressed through fertility
rites and by the cyclic appearance, disappearance, and reap-
pearance of a god, do not rest their truth claims upon the
historical actuality of a dying and reviving god, for the fertility gods and heroes are significant as surrogates for natural
forces rather than as historical individuals. With Christianity,
however, God is primarily met in history, in the timely events
and relationships there experienced by men.

From the point of view of Christian faith and Christian
theology, it is clear that there must be an objective event or
events behind the New Testament narratives, or else the
faith as it has been historically known is destroyed. The
relevance to human life of the Scriptural treatment of the in-

carnation is either rooted in history or it is a platitude. If there is not an essential historicity in the New Testament accounts of the life, death, and resurrection of Jesus Christ, we are, as the apostle Paul said, of all men most deceived. Prof. Richard R. Niebuhr makes the point in his recent study *Resurrection and Historical Reason* when he writes that "no amount of patching with the concepts of hero and of immortality can make a unity of the history again, once the passion and death are surrendered through the dissolution of the resurrection as the key to the meaning of the New Testament."[4] Other approaches to the passion and the resurrection do not succeed in making the New Testament faith either credible or intelligible, and may result only in making it sentimental and nostalgic.

Now if historical understanding is to be preserved, and if it is to be made known effectively to large numbers of persons, then it must be preserved in a form of writing which is, in the words of one of our leading historical dramatists, "sufficiently dramatic to attract a crowd." More is involved than a set of archives and more is required than scholarly reports of the events, minutely documented, for such reports would attract but little attention beyond a restricted circle of specialists. If, as Christians believe, certain historical events and certain historical understandings are relevant to *all* men, then these must be conveyed in a manner which can reach and affect all sorts and conditions of men. The literary treatments must thus accomplish a twofold objective: to be basically faithful to the events treated and to be potentially affective with the wide audience addressed. And I assume that these objectives, among others, are attributable to the authors of the books of Scripture.

These two objectives are also two of the objectives of a certain type of dramatic history which is represented, for example, by Shakespeare's *King Richard II*. To be sure, there are differences as well as similarities involved. Thus, the Shakespearean poetry is essentially concerned with beauty in a way in which the Christian Scriptures are not. Furthermore, as we have already said, the Christian faith is dependent on historical events in a way in which Shakespearean art is not. Although Shakespeare, when he was treating the history of his own country, was particularly faithful to the history he knew, it is centrally important for us to remember that the mirror which he held up to life in *Richard II* would be equally valuable to us regardless of whether or not Richard lived and was king of England, whereas the same stable value would surely not apply to the Christian view of life, regardless of whether or not Jesus lived and was the incarnate Son of God. The difference lies in the fact that, for the Christian, salvation comes through what God *did* in Christ in reconciling man to himself, rather than just in what Christ said or in what was said about him. If the incarnation did not occur in the historical events of the life, death, and resurrection of Jesus Christ, then the Christian gospel is dissolved within the recurrent cycles of the myth of renewal. It is true that the life of Christ as presented in the New Testament in some measure adumbrates the renewal patterns (though not so extensively as is sometimes maintained), but by the very fact that it was a historical event it obviates the essential frustration involved in those endlessly repeated patterns. Man as man can never ultimately succeed in his attempts at renewal through ritual, nor through his cathartic participation in tragedy, as a later development of ritual, for he must endlessly repeat the ritual and the tragedy for such partial expiation, catharsis, or triumph as may come to him from them. But whatever comes is always partial and always needs to be itself renewed. The claim of Christianity is that a unique historical event has broken the pattern of a perennial need for renewal. And if the event were not essentially historical, that central Christian claim is false. The Sermon on the Mount may be true regardless of whether Christ lived, but the Christian drama of man's salvation is inextricably dependent upon time, place, and personality "under Pontius Pilate." If God did not act in history in Jesus Christ, it may still be true that men are sinful and that this is a bad thing, but in the distinctively and uniquely Christian sense there will be no escape from that fact.

This distinction as to content between the New Testament and the Shakespearean treatments of history is necessary and central, but once it has been clearly made we should go on to notice as parallel to this distinction of content a similarity of form. Both secular and sacred writers must employ certain standard literary devices if history is to be made lastingly and meaningfully relevant to audiences removed in space and time and cultural identity from the original happenings. When a serious dramatic writer, as distinguished from a serious professional historian, attempts to draw up a faithful dramatic representation of historical characters and events, he does so in terms of certain rather well defined literary techniques. In fact, these techniques provide virtually the only way in which the existence and significance of historical characters may be preserved and communicated affectively and honestly to large numbers of people. The techniques would seem to apply to the New Testament in much the same way that they apply to *Richard II*, even though the particular validity, or lack of validity, of Shakespeare's drama is *not* determined by what happened in late fourteenth-century England while the particular validity, or lack of validity, of the Christian evangel *is* determined by what happened in early first-century Palestine.

What I mean by the techniques necessary for the serious literary and dramatic treatment of history may be indicated in connection with three historical dramas: Robert Sherwood's *Abe Lincoln in Illinois,* William Shakespeare's *Richard II,* and George Bernard Shaw's *Saint Joan.**

Each of these plays represents a meaningful literary and dramatic treatment of events and persons within a framework of responsible regard for what happened in the first place. Thus when Robert Sherwood wrote *Abe Lincoln in Illinois,* it was with the expressed conviction that "a strict regard for the plain truth is more than obligatory; it is obviously desirable."[5] At the same time Sherwood declared that he was writing neither as a scholarly recorder of facts nor as an exact reporter. The dramatist's stock in trade is feeling rather than facts, and when he treats history "he is, at best, an interpreter, with a certain facility for translating all that he has heard in a manner sufficiently dramatic to attract a crowd."[6]

Let us note first that Sherwood treats the events of his history in terms of their value for illuminating the character of Lincoln. In the short space of time available for a stage play—you could read through an average stage play in about the same length of time that you would need for reading the Gospel of Luke—there must of necessity be a great deal of condensation. What is told must be highly effective for its purposes, in order to justify its inclusion at all, and thus most of what happens to a person must be omitted entirely. At the same time, Sherwood may heighten the effectiveness of his treatment by distortions of fact—as when he has Lincoln reading Dickens' *Pickwick Papers* a year before they were

* Each of these three writers clearly intends to give a historically responsible presentation of the characters and events which are treated in these particular plays, and in this fact their approach is markedly different from that of popular "historical" novels. By and large, the popular historical novel plays fast and loose with history, using the past for exotic setting and stimulus. The past provides a backdrop of mystery, color, pageantry, glamour, and adventure, but there is generally no very serious attempt to present a faithful account of historic events and characters. At least in the more popular works, then, we may say that historical fiction generally has no more concern for history than science fiction has for science.

published, or meeting his good friend Joshua Speed two or three years earlier than was actually the case. He also pictures Lincoln reading Keats' "On Death," although we have no evidence whatsoever of Lincoln's ever having known the poem at all. But by each of these devices—each of which represents a distortion of fact—he makes what he calls "a steadfast effort to reflect the character of Lincoln as truthfully as I can."[7] To the same end, Sherwood uses the various historical characters who cluster around Lincoln, "not as people important in themselves but as sources of light, each one being present only for the purpose of casting a beam to illumine some one of the innumerable facets of Lincoln's spirit."[8] It is only by the use of such devices as these that it would be possible to present in the time and form available an interpretation of Lincoln which is at once faithful, meaningful, and convincing to sizable numbers of people.

So it was with Shakespeare's interpretation of the English King Richard II. Here Shakespeare was dealing with a monarch whom he wished to treat with particular historical care, and he did so with such effectiveness that the leading twentieth-century authority on the reign of Richard II, Prof. Vivian Galbraith, of Oxford, has declared Shakespeare's portrayal to be about as close to the mark as it is possible to come.[9] But this does not mean that Shakespeare's treatment of historical events and characters in *Richard II* is a piece of strictly accurate reporting. The ages of individual characters are altered, events are placed in closer chronological relationship than that in which they occurred, and chronology is otherwise altered to varying degrees. The result is a characterization which is substantially correct, from a historical point of view, despite its purposeful alteration of historical detail, and which has been able to "attract a crowd" far longer than any other treatment of the same subject.

When we come to George Bernard Shaw's *Saint Joan* we find again the same general pattern of treatment. Shaw admits to making the same types of alteration we have already observed in Sherwood and Shakespeare, and he justifies these changes as the necessary sacrifice of verisimilitude in order to achieve veracity. The words "verisimilitude" and "veracity" here are significant, verisimilitude meaning the reproduction of events exactly as in a replica, and veracity meaning what Shaw calls "essential truth." This "essential truth" to history is portrayed dramatically through an occasionally "inexact picture of some accidental facts." It is by "this inevitable sacrifice of verisimilitude," Shaw writes, that "I have secured in the only possible way sufficient veracity" to justify claiming to understand the history treated and to communicate that understanding to audiences removed from any specialized concern with the historical persons involved. Shaw candidly admits that he has accorded his characters a larger understanding of the issues involved in their lives than they could possibly have possessed while the historical events were taking place. Thus his Earl of Warwick clearly sees that Joan's appeal to a national loyalty under the King, rather than to the conventional feudal loyalty to the lord of her manor, can spell the death of the feudal system and of the baronial class of which he is the spokesman. Similarly, the Roman Catholic dignitaries who try Joan see in her direct appeal to the revealed will of God, apart from the mediatorial offices of the church, a threat to the very foundations of the Roman Church, a threat far more fearful than any petty suspicion of witchcraft. Thus, the bishop calls Joan a Protestant, while the earl calls her a Nationalist—terms which neither of them were in a chronological position to use or even to know. But Shaw denies that the result is falsification. What he has done, as he says, is to sacrifice verisimilitude for veracity, and he rightly declares that the sacrifice is both necessary and inevitable. "It is the business of the stage," he writes, "to make its figures more intelligible to themselves than they would be in real life; for by no other means can they be made intelligible to the audience."[10]

What we have here, then, are the techniques of *dramatic history*. All events are not given a place in the story, the chronological order of the events which are included is sometimes changed, particular incidents are repeated or conflated with other incidents, and characters are endowed with an understanding which may have been present only in embryo at the time of the events treated. Now this description of the manner of operation within the form of dramatic history will not seem unfamiliar, for much the same manner of operation is present in the Gospels.

It will not come as news to any reader that the various New Testament accounts of history at certain points differ and disagree. Although the points of disagreement do not crucially affect the central New Testament message, they are nonetheless quite apparent and may be quite misleading unless they are understood within some such context as that of dramatic history. Matthew, Mark, Luke, and John do not concur as to the chronology of Jesus' ministry, as to the precise length of that ministry, or as to the place within it of certain events such as, for example, the cleansing of the Temple. The Beatitudes as reported by Luke are not the same as those reported by Matthew, and Matthew draws together many of Jesus' teachings into the Sermon on the Mount, while Luke treats his rather similar and yet different compend as the Sermon on the Plain. There are often variations in the reported words of Jesus on what is clearly the same occasion, as for example in Jesus' rebuke of the sleeping Peter in Gethsemane, for which Matthew, Mark, and Luke provide different versions.

So we find operative in the New Testament the same

methods which we have observed in the dramatic histories.
It could scarcely be otherwise. As Donald Baillie has written,
a photographic portrait of Jesus would not provide us with
the most true or the most real acquaintance with him, and
we will generally recognize, I suppose, that the accounts of
Jesus' life were all written under the light of Easter and
Pentecost, as indeed they should have been. The interaction
between event and interpretation, between fact and meaning,
indicates the affinity between the Gospel narratives and the
techniques of dramatic history. Thus when Professor Knox
writes of "infidelity to fact for the sake of fidelity to meaning," and when he says that, since the risen Christ is as real
as Jesus of Nazareth, it is not absolutely essential to locate
precise words and acts within the historical and "objective"
career of Jesus, he is speaking in terms of the principle of
dramatic history.[11] This principle may be defined as the sacrifice of verisimilitude in order to maintain veracity.* Without

---

* One further operation of the same principle may be seen in the dramatic
dialogues through which Socrates is presented by Plato, who was, we must
remember, as great a literary figure as he was a philosopher. In his study of
Socrates, Prof. A. E. Taylor makes clear that Socrates' life and teachings have
been popularly preserved, as he puts it, only by "the Providence which gave
him a younger friend and follower" who was capable of re-creating his life
through literary techniques (Socrates, p. 130). But that Plato re-created the
life of Socrates through his writings should not be taken to imply that he
created it. Modern attitudes toward Socrates have developed from the nine-
teenth-century theory of the "historical Socrates"—by which was meant,
Professor Taylor tells us, "the Socrates of Plato with the genius taken out of
him"—through a "complete skepticism about the very possibility of any
knowledge of the 'historical Socrates' " which led Diels to refer to him as the
"unknown x"—a phrase, as well as a development, which will again strike
New Testament students as familiar—to the position which Taylor and others
now generally hold. "Of course it is not suggested," according to Professor
Taylor, "that all Plato's Socratic dialogues are close reports of actual conversations, like those recorded by Boswell, though it is likely enough that
some of them are founded on actual conversations. What is meant is simply
that the dialogues intend to exhibit a faithful picture of the situation, interests, and views of a real historical man" (Socrates, pp. 16, 17, and 27. Thomas
Nelson & Sons, 1939). Again we see operative the principles governing the
form of dramatic history—not verisimilitude, but veracity.

it, history cannot for long be preserved in a literary form which is at once faithful, vital, and meaningful to generations of men.

II. *"Myth" and Symbol*

Such a preservation of history is of far greater importance for Christianity than for the other world religions, since the Christian Scriptures are basically concerned with man's relations to God, to his neighbor, and to himself in the context of history, and since the Christian faith proclaims God's redemption of man through historical action, rather than through otherworldly and "mystical" exercises. But the Christian Scriptures are concerned with more than the recounting of history, and frequently use stories not based in history so as to make clear to man the issues and challenges involved in his historical existence. Poets and literary critics alike have repeatedly cited the literary greatness of Scripture, and specifically Christian writers such as Boccaccio and Sidney have pointedly emphasized the fact that literary form was the chosen vehicle of truth in Scripture. Thus Boccaccio defended fiction by referring to the fact that "Christ, who is God, used this sort of fiction again and again in his parables,"[12] while Sidney argued for the superiority of literary concreteness over philosophical abstraction by reference to the practice of Christ:

> Certainly even our Savior Christ could as well have given the moral commonplaces of uncharitableness and humbleness as the divine narration of Dives and Lazarus; or of disobedience and mercy as that heavenly discourse of the lost child and the gracious father; but that his through-searching wisdom knew the estate of Dives burning in hell and of Lazarus being in Abraham's bosom, would more constantly (as it were) inhabit both the memory and the judgment.[13]

Again, then, literature provides the means by which ultimate insights will "inhabit both the memory and the judgment." The Christian faith, as preserved in Scripture, communicates itself not only through dramatic history but also through literary images, metaphors, and stories. This fact can scarcely be denied, but it may be ignored, and when it is ignored the result is an inevitable oversimplification. Within the past hundred years, I would suggest, the oversimplification has taken two distinctive forms—fundamentalism and demythologizing. It may seem strange to link these two schools together as I am doing, but from the literary point of view they represent the two different sides of the same coin. Both are reductionist, though their reductionism operates in opposite directions. Neither seems able to accept literary symbols as such, and they insist upon reducing the literary either to the literal or to the ideational.

With the loss of a properly literary understanding of symbol and story, fundamentalism delivered itself up to misrepresentation and in no small measure delivered the Scriptures themselves up to popular misunderstanding. From this historical fact, above all others, stemmed the decline of the influence of Scripture upon the lives, thoughts, and imaginations of men. Faced with fundamentalist assertions of the literal infallibility of all Biblical statements, and with the equally erroneous alternative that if the Scriptures are not literally true in all parts then they are not true at all, many men of honest mind repudiated the Scriptures. In these and other ways, fundamentalism was idolatrous of the written words of Scripture, and at the same time denied literary reality as well as scientific and historical demonstrations. Had there been a fuller recognition of the literary approaches to truth through symbol, metaphor, and parable, Christianity might have been spared the entire fundamentalist debacle.

The fundamentalist distortion has been repeatedly exposed

and is certainly on the wane today, although some fundamentalist factions still survive. For our own generation, the
major reductionism is found in another quarter, but again
it involves a basic misunderstanding of the relevant literary
approaches to truth. Having escaped from the danger of reducing the symbolic to the literal, we now find ourselves
deeply involved in the similar danger of reducing the symbolic to the abstract. Prof. Amos Wilder, of Harvard, thus
warns against the demythologizing approach to Scripture
which seeks "a clear idea in imaginative discourse," which
proceeds by method of "an undue abstraction of the full-
bodied symbolic discourse" in order to arrive at "a wisdom
that can be identified with some prose statement or some theological formula."[14] Such a procedure is based upon highly
questionable semantic decisions, and in reality amounts to an
abstracting of living imagery into cryptophilosophical ab-
stractions, as Wilder and others have shown.

Our concern in this first chapter is with the relevance of
methods of general literary exegesis to theological endeavor.
We are concerned, in other words, with hermeneutic method
and, as Prof. Rudolf Bultmann has said, demythologizing is
in reality "an hermeneutic method, that is, a method of interpretation, of exegesis."[15] Certain very important literary
principles, which are relevant to the entire range of theological endeavor, may be illustrated by reference to the demythologizing issue, as it has been raised by Professor Bultmann.

A number of difficulties are present in any discussion of
demythologizing. First of all there is the question of the
meaning of the word "myth" itself. There are, indeed, so
many definitions of myth incident to particular individuals,
schools of thought, and academic disciplines, that the word
actually has no *public* meaning, even among scholars. If we
try to collate the uses assigned to it in recent years in the writings of Cassirer, Langer, Malinowski, Campbell, Raglan,

Jung, Reik, Fromm, Foss, Chase, Hamilton, Harrison, Zimmer, Weisinger, Levy, Frankfort, and Bultmann, we will find that various meanings overlap and intersect, conflict and contradict, in very interesting but decidedly confusing ways. On the basis of this semantic confusion, I seriously doubt that scholarly discussion will be much clarified by using the term, and would personally prefer to abandon it altogether.

We must, nevertheless, take up the discussion where it is. For our purposes here, then, "myth" will be used in Professor Bultmann's sense as a mode of thinking in which the divine appears as the human and the otherworldly as this-worldly, although this by no means represents the inevitable meaning of the term, and most contemporary scholars have given quite different definitions. Among British and American critics of the first rank, only Paul Elmer More, so far as I have been able to discover, used this definition prior to the discussion which Professor Bultmann has initiated, and Professor More warned against demythologizing by any philosophical "juggling of terms."[16] Finally, I must confess that I for one find Professor Bultmann's own usage far from clear, and am considerably confused, for example, by the fact that his definitions allow him to treat the pre-existent Christ as a myth, the resurrection of Christ as a myth, and yet to hold that he is speaking in demythologized terms when he says that "Christ is not merely a past phenomenon, but the ever-present word of God."[17] At this and other similar points it appears to me that the real and undeniable value of Bultmann's exegesis lies in inconsistency and in his tacit violation of his own system.

Having made these necessary qualifications, we can proceed to set up a frame of literary reference by which to judge either the reductionism of Bultmann or the reductionism of the fundamentalists. This frame of reference may be found in the understanding of symbol, metaphor, and story which has been basic to the history of literary creation and analysis.

It has value as a method which goes far beyond its contemporary relevance to fundamentalism and demythologizing. For our purposes here we will consider this method in terms of three broad principles: first the principle of accommodation or of entasis to which we will now turn, then the principle which Coleridge described as the "willing suspension of disbelief," and finally the principle of a distinctive validity which characterizes certain literary uses.

A. *Accommodation of God's Truth*

It is of primary importance to recognize that literary truth involves truth to the human situation, broadly conceived, rather than accuracy of factual detail. "Fact is not too important," William Faulkner has said, "but truth is the constant thing."[18] Robert Louis Stevenson put the case for literary truth when he wrote that "to tell the truth, rightly understood, is not to state the true facts, but to convey a true impression; truth in spirit, not truth to the letter, is the true veracity."[19] And in that statement we will of course recognize the Pauline admonition that "the letter killeth, but the spirit giveth life."[20] Again, Goethe spoke to the same effect when he wrote that "truth in Nature and truth in Art are quite different things."[21]

We could go on indefinitely expanding citations on this point, but it might be more useful to cite instead a parallel situation in another field. Greek architects long ago discovered that if a column were carved absolutely straight, it would give the optical illusion of being curved in upon itself. Experience demonstrated that if a column were to appear straight to onlookers, it could not be straight, but must be given an outward swelling curve, which was called entasis. Thus, Greek "columns were carved so that they swelled to-

ward the middle and then diminished in diameter." Furthermore "the axes of the columns in a well-designed Greek temple were slightly inclined inward, so as to counteract the
tendency which a vertical column has to appear to lean out-
wards."[22] Now this architectural distortion of straightness in
order to give the appearance of straightness is directly relevant
to what we have been saying about literary uses of fiction as
a means of conveying truth. If we wish to borrow a Greek
aesthetic term to apply to this process, we may then call it the
process of entasis.

In this chapter we are interested in literary method as it
contributes to theological understanding, and so we should
move on from the principle of entasis as it is applied in human art to the theory of accommodation as it has been applied to divine revelation. It is intensely unfortunate, I think,
that the doctrine of accommodation has lost the prominent
place it once held in Christian theology, especially in the
theology of Calvin. For Calvin, as Professor Dowey has said,
"the principle of accommodation always intervenes" between God and man's knowledge of God. Dowey gives this
brief definition of the term: "Accommodation refers to the
process by which God reduces or adjusts to human capacities
what he wills to reveal of the infinite mysteries of his being,
which by their very nature are beyond the powers of the
mind of man to grasp."[23]

It was in terms of the broader implications of this theory of
accommodation that Calvin urbanely dealt with certain types
of difficulty in the Scriptures which in later centuries fundamentalist interpreters were to erect into major stumbling
blocks to honesty. Even in Calvin's time, at least one passage
early in Genesis was recognized as running counter to scientific knowledge, and this was the reference to the moon as
one of the two great lights of heaven. In treating this passage
in his commentary on Genesis, Calvin set himself in direct
opposition to fundamentalism by flatly denying the literal

accuracy of the Biblical description and asserting that "astronomers prove" a literal interpretation of the Biblical statement to be scientifically false. He then proceeded to praise the great value of scientific investigation, even such scientific investigation as this which runs counter to the literal expression of Scripture: "Such study is certainly not to be disapproved, nor science condemned with the insolence of some fanatics who habitually reject whatever is unknown to them." On the contrary, "clever men who expend their labor upon it are to be praised and those who have ability and leisure ought not to neglect work of that kind."[24]

The scientific inaccuracy of Genesis is irrelevant here, for, as Calvin says in applying the theory of accommodation, "Moses adapts himself to the ordinary view" so as to convey the nonscientific truth which is his real concern. This truth is that "God has stretched out his hand to us to give us the splendor of the sun and moon to enjoy. Great would be our ingratitude if we shut our eyes to this experience of beauty!" In "the nightly splendor of the moon" we are to "recognize the goodness of God."[25] Thus in Calvin's interpretation of Scripture we find scientific error used to present divine truth through literary means. Calvin was making use of the perennial literary principle which Robert Louis Stevenson was later to describe when he wrote, as we have already noted, that "to tell the truth, rightly understood, is not to state the true facts, but to convey a true impression; truth in spirit, not truth to the letter, is the true veracity." To this principle, whether we refer to it as the principle of entasis or of accommodation, we will often return, as it is central to the entire enterprise of literature.

That this principle destroys the very bases of a literalist theology is so patent as not to require further comment. It is important, however, to indicate in some detail how accommodation differs from the demythologizing proposed by Prof. Rudolf Bultmann. In the first place, accommodation abides

by the original symbols and works through them, whereas
demythologizing would replace the original symbols and
myths with an abstracted and contemporaneously structured
idea. Even more basic, however, is the fact that as traditionally applied in Christian exegesis, accommodation has accepted the presence of an objective reality behind the symbol,
whereas, in general, demythologizing does not seem to do
so. Prof. Amos Wilder summarizes Bultmann's attitude as
follows:

> Bultmann's rationalist legacy . . . makes it impossible for him
> to recognize the true character of myth. Myth for him is only
> time-conditioned, pre-scientific error. True it suggests man's
> understanding of his "existence" (understanding "existence"
> here in the special sense given it in existential philosophy).
> But this is all. It carries no truth. The myth of the Redeemer
> carries no truth. The myth of vicarious redemption carries no
> truth. The myth of world-judgment and a new age carries no
> truth.[26]

As against that conception, Wilder states a fundamental objection, and in doing so he indicates the general direction in
which the interpretations of accommodation may move:

> The basic problem is not one of obsolete conceptions, but of
> the very language of religion and its interpretation. It is a
> problem of semantics. We are dealing with mythopoetic lan-
> guage and our problem is to understand what it tells us. We
> are dealing with the imaginative language of faith to be inter-
> preted, not with dead myths.[27]

Here Wilder has posed an objection which, from a purely
literary point of view, seems to be not only quite sound but
even irrefutable.

An even more forceful statement comes from John Milton,
in which as a Christian thinker and poet he repudiates the reductionism by which Biblical metaphor, symbol, and parable
may be replaced by a "fundamentalist" and literal interpreta-

tion or by an abstract and "demythologized" understanding of the Scriptural treatment of God:

> Our safest way is to form in our minds such a conception of God, as shall correspond with his own delineation and representation of himself in the sacred writings. For granting that both in the literal and figurative descriptions of God, he is exhibited not as he really is, but in such a manner as may be within the scope of our comprehensions, yet we ought to entertain such a conception of him, as he, in condescending to accommodate himself to our capacities, has shown that he desires we should conceive. For it is on this very account that he has lowered himself to our level, lest in our flights above the reach of human understanding, and beyond the written word of Scripture, we should be tempted to indulge in vague cogitations and subtleties.[28]

The doctrine of accommodation, then, clearly posits a reality behind the symbols, and holds that, although the symbols in some measure distort that reality, they do so only in order to bring it within the reach of man.

B. *Faith, and the Suspension of Disbelief*

We must turn now to a second important principle in the literary approach to truth, and this principle is summed up in Samuel Taylor Coleridge's well-known phrase: the "willing suspension of disbelief." This willing suspension of disbelief is a radically different thing from Christian faith, which is not a suspension of disbelief but a commitment of life in reliance upon God. Faith, as Luther graphically defined it, is a lively, reckless confidence in the grace of God. Literarily, on the other hand, willing suspension of disbelief is the choice to enter into communication with a literary document, the willingness to listen to it as it speaks in its own terms. If such a writer as Milton or the prophet Ezekiel has dealt largely in accommodation and entasis, then we must for a period at least suspend our disbelief in following his narrative or in concentrating upon his symbols. It is not that we need to believe a lie—as Boccaccio put it, the serious writer "has nothing in common with any variety of falsehood, for it is not a poet's purpose to deceive anybody with his inventions," it being on the contrary his purpose to lead us to truth.[29]

As we approach the literary document, however, we must admit the scheme and the action which it uses in order to understand what it would say, and only then are we in a position to appraise it in a measured and judicious acceptance or rejection. The willing suspension of disbelief is precisely what Calvin practiced when he read the account of Jesus' baptism where it is said that the heavens opened and the Spirit of God descended in the likeness of a dove and lighted on him. Calvin comments that, although John the Baptist "says that he saw the Holy Spirit descending," what he actually saw was not the Holy Spirit at all, but only a dove. That is disbelief in the outward form of the action, but this disbelief is suspended in the sense in which we use the term as Calvin proceeds to understand that the action symbolizes the real presence of the Spirit of God in Christ, represented to John by accommodation according to his capacity.[30]

As for the relevance of this principle of the "willing suspension of disbelief" to demythologizing, two things should be said. In the first place, there can only be hearty endorsement of Bultmann's denial that the message of Scripture is as obsolete as its science. But, in the second place, we must note that Bultmann has introduced nonliterary criteria into his hermeneutics when he allows his literary exegesis to be determined by his assumption that, as he says, "modern man acknowledges as reality only such phenomena or events as are comprehensible within the framework of the rational order of the universe."[31]

A parallel to Bultmann's position vis-à-vis Scriptural symbols may be found by referring to a contention advanced some half century ago that Milton's *Paradise Lost* is a monument to dead ideas. Even among those who would agree with this appraisal, however, there are so far as I know none among literarily responsible critics who would therefore see Milton's epic "demythologized." By strictly literary standards, to "demythologize" or to "translate" any literary work into symbols other than its own would be to destroy it.

A literary work *is* its own meaning, and its meaning cannot be univocally abstracted from it. This is the one literary principle upon which all competent literary critics now agree. It appears to me that Bultmann destroys the validity of his position when he directly contradicts this universal principle, as he does when he declares of "mythological" symbols and images that "their meaning can and must be stated without recourse to mythological terms."[32]

C. *Validation of This Truth*

We are now in a position to see that a third principle emerges from the operation of the first two principles which we have been discussing. As the symbols produced under the principle of accommodation interact with each other and are considered in terms of the willing suspension of disbelief, a distinctive kind of validity is evolved. A method is at work here which, though fundamentally different from logical or mathematical or scientific or historical demonstration, nonetheless provides for its own ordered progression of thought.

In connection with this third principle of distinctive validity we may note John Calvin's Christian humanist assertion about symbols that "there is no need for the reality to agree at all points with the symbol, if only it suit sufficiently for the purpose of symbolizing."[33] As an illustration of the operation of this principle we may cite John Milton's use of an outdated cosmology in *Paradise Lost.* Although Milton knew, as the ancient Hebrews did not, that the ancient divisions of space were not scientifically valid, he continued to use the old symbol because "there is no need for the reality to agree at all points with the symbol, if only it suit sufficiently for the purpose of symbolizing."

This matter of cosmology brings us to one of the clearest test cases in the current discussions of demythologizing—the symbol of the spatial elevation of God above the earth. Let us examine this issue, beginning with Milton's deliberate employment of spatial symbols in *Paradise Lost.* Milton knew Galileo personally, visited with him, and was quite aware of the fact that the old three-storied view of the universe was under serious and mortal attack as scientifically unacceptable. Indeed, Milton was just as unwilling as is Professor Bultmann in our own day to affirm univocally that God is located spatially "up there, above us."* In *Paradise Lost* he flatly declares that the relationship of God to man, heaven to earth, are in

> distance inexpressible
> By numbers that have name.[34]

---

* In the century just before Milton's, John Calvin had warned against "a careful and literal interpretation" of the spatial metaphors and remarked caustically that "when we say Christ is in heaven, we must not imagine that he is somewhere among the cosmic spheres, counting the stars!" We use such images because they are appropriate, and we do not abandon them because they are not replicas of God's reality. "In other words," Calvin continues, "when God is said to be in heaven, it is not meant that he is inside it; we must remember the words, 'Heaven of heavens do not contain him' (II Chron. 2:6). This expression sets him apart from all creatures, and warns us that no mean and earthy thoughts about him should enter our minds, because he is higher than the whole world." At the same time, "we must speak of the Kingdom of God using the only language which we have." (*Calvin-Commentaries,* trans. and ed. Joseph Haroutunian, pp. 174, 286, and 174. The Westminster Press, 1958.)

Professor Bultmann himself could have no objection to such a view—but he does object to using space as a "myth" for putting God in a distance-relationship to man. Milton, without attaching any literal or replica quality to the metaphor, nonetheless proceeds to make it one of the basic "myths" of his epic. Bultmann, denying its literal or replica quality, would do away with it. In Bultmann's view, one of the things which makes demythologizing necessary is the expression of "the transcendence of God in terms of remoteness in space."[35] Milton, steeped as he was in classical learning, would probably have replied to such an objection by asking, in some bewilderment, why the notion of God as expressed by Professor Bultmann in the word "transcendent" is more acceptable than the notion of God as "above," since the word "transcendent" is merely a frozen metaphor from the Latin for that which is above.

The same point was made in the Gifford Lectures for 1933–1934 by the late Prof. Edwyn Bevan, who discussed spatial symbolism at great length and concluded that there is no satisfactory way to avoid such symbols, for they invariably creep back into a discussion in terms of such hidden spatial metaphors as "transcend," "excel," or "superior."[36] And if God is going to be "pointed out" as it were, even though covertly, then the basic question is as to the meaning of the direction in which one points. The Hebrew-Christian tradition has generally been to point symbolically above; the Indian tradition, of Hinduism and Buddhism, has primarily pointed symbolically within. In each tradition, of course, there has been some pointing in both directions, and these tendencies may be variously explained, but the fact remains that the basic Hindu-Buddhist tendency has been to look for God *within*, while the basic Biblical tendency has been to look *above*. The difference is not accidental and ornamental, but is fundamental and definitive. For Milton, as for the

Christian tradition generally, the use of the upward and downward separation of God and man served as an unpassable metaphoric bulwark against any monist identification of man with God.

And there are of course other meanings. The upwardness of heaven and downwardness of hell are fraught with an implicit meaning which is clear enough in terms of metaphoric thought, and which is made explicit in Bunyan's *Pilgrim's Progress* when one of the younger pilgrims says that "the way to Heaven is as up a Ladder, and the way to Hell is as down a Hill."[37] The same conception is embodied in *Paradise Lost* in the bridge which is built by Sin and Death, Satan's off-spring and partners in an unholy infernal trinity, to join earth and hell: "a passage broad, Smooth, easy, inoffensive down to Hell."[38] Image and meaning are clear, and we are not required to believe cosmologically in a three-storied universe in order to understand. Nor do the facts of astronomy, with which Milton was basically familiar enough, invalidate the image, for Milton was not writing a poem about astronomy and physics, but about man's life here and hereafter. And he did it in the only way in which it has ever been possible to write a lastingly meaningful treatment of his subject, that is, in terms of metaphor and symbol, or, to use the currently fashionable word, slippery though it may be, in terms of "myth." In sum, Milton was concerned neither with a geocentric nor with a heliocentric view of the cosmos, but rather with a theocentric view of man's existence.

Dante was, of course, bound to the Ptolemaic, geocentric view of the universe in a way which Milton was not, for scientific endeavor had offered Dante no alternative to it, but he too made it clear that his symbols, images, and narratives did not represent literal replicas of the realities to which he referred. In a memorable treatment of God's "infinite excess" he writes:

> Each lesser measure, then, if thou perpend,
> Is a too scant receptacle for that Good
> Which is its own measure, and hath no end.[39]

Words are just as "scant" as any other "receptacles," for

> The passing beyond bounds of human sense
> Words cannot tell; let then the example sate
> Him for whom grace reserves the experience.[40]

Again the point is clear: transcendence is best treated by example. "Let then the example" be enough, Dante would say, and do not reduce it either to abstraction or to literalism. Like Dante and Milton, John Bunyan also holds to the validity of the metaphorical approach. By using "one thing to set forth another," he says, he is but following the practice of the Scriptures in using the most effective means of communication, for metaphor and simile

> Will stick faster in the heart and head
> Than things from similes not borrowed.[41]

An excellent example of the operation of a distinctive literary or metaphorical logic may be found in John Milton's story of Satan, Sin, Death, and the Hell-hounds, a story which Milton creates so as to lay bare the anatomy of the problem of evil as he understands it. In this instance, Milton treats man's relationship to evil in terms of proliferating personal relationships. Following the traditional Christian symbols, he begins with the titanic and protean figure of Satan, who had existed in heaven as the archangel Lucifer, second only to the divine, but who concludes that to be first among angelic creatures is not enough, determines to overthrow the Almighty, and attempts to make himself God. In the very process of hatching this "bold conspiracy against Heav'n's King" he finds his head struck with "miserable pain" as there springs forth from his forehead a seductive female figure called Sin, in whom he recognizes his own "perfect image." Having conceived and projected the idea of his own divinity in the figure of Sin, Satan becomes enamored of her. An incestuous union ensues, as Satan seals the acceptance of his own ultimacy by becoming metaphorically "one flesh" with Sin.

In that action, Satan repudiates his existence as a creature, chooses to end the life of Lucifer, prince of light, and henceforth becomes Satan, prince of darkness. As the death of Lucifer results from the consummation of his union with Sin, metaphorically understood, so as a result of that union Sin gives birth to Death itself, personifying the inevitable destruction of the value of life which follows upon the embracing of Sin. Satan's new existence is now defined in terms of new categories, as he has made inescapable the condition which he himself summarizes in the words "myself am Hell" and upon which Milton comments that Hell

> boils in his tumultuous breast,
> And like a devilish engine back recoils
> Upon himself; horror and doubt distract
> His troubl'd thoughts, and from the bottom stir
> The Hell within him, for within him Hell
> He brings, and round about him, nor from Hell
> One step no more than from himself can fly
> By change of place.[42]

Prior to the birth of Death, Sin had seemed entirely fair, but as she brings forth Death her figure becomes distorted into a double aspect, still partly seductive but also now partly revolting, so that she appears

> Woman to the waist, and fair,
> But ended foul in many a scaly fold
> Voluminous and vast, a serpent arm'd
> With mortal sting.[43]

The two apparitions, Sin and Death, sit as gatekeepers to Hell, and look upon one another: Sin in revulsion at what she sees, but Death in insatiable hunger until, terrified of his own barren emptiness, he rapes his mother in a fury of lust and hate. This rape too is inevitable because Sin, personifying the finite assertion of infinity, exerts upon Death, the personification of inescapable finitude, a violent attraction compounded of lust, envy, and hate. From the union of these two figures, in what Sin calls "embraces forcible and foul," are born innumerable particular sins symbolized by the little monsters called Hell-hounds. Up until this time, Sin had been original and undivided, but now she brings forth the myriads of individual sins which inevitably result from the rape by Death of finitude's sinful pretension to infinity. Sin can neither separate herself from her offspring nor find joy in them, but can only endure the torture which they inflict upon her. She describes them to Satan as

> These yelling monsters that with ceaseless cry
> Surround me, as thou saw'st, hourly conceiv'd
> And hourly born, with sorrow infinite
> To me, for when they list into the womb
> That bred them they return, and howl and gnaw
> My bowels, their repast; then bursting forth
> Afresh with conscious terrors vex me round,
> That rest or intermission none I find.[44]

When Satan comes to the gates of Hell, and first sees the Hell-hounds, with their parents and his children Sin and Death, he declares in revulsion that he never "saw till now Sight more detestable,"[45] but when he realizes that these are the natural offspring of his own assumption of ultimacy, he hails them as his "fair" children. To repudiate them, or to repudiate Hell, would be to repudiate his own infinite pretension, which Satan steadfastly refuses to do. To maintain

that pretension, he must inevitably accept its correlates in
Sin, Death, the Hell-hounds, and Hell.

The entire progression of this parable is inevitable, because
there is at work in it a distinctive form of method and logic.
It is not, to be sure, the logic of philosophy or the method of
mathematical reasoning, but it is an equally coherent logic
of images which moves from one figure to another in a closely
knit and inherently ordered progression of understanding.
Granted the originating sin, all the rest follows without inter-
mission and without the slightest possibility of evasion.

The distinctive validity of literary symbols may be further
illustrated by the analysis of a passage from one of Hamlet's
best-known soliloquies:

> To be, or not to be—that is the question:
> Whether 'tis nobler in the mind to suffer
> The slings and arrows of outrageous fortune
> Or to take arms against a sea of troubles,
> And by opposing end them.[46]

The opening line clearly poses an "existential question"—
"To be or not to be"—and the entire passage considers this
question "existentially." But it does not consider it philo-
sophically or scientifically. Hamlet's words are absurd if taken
in any but a metaphorical sense. Who could "take arms
against a sea"? What weapon could possibly be effective in
fighting the tide? We cannot hope to understand Hamlet
here until we accept the fact that his thoughts move in terms
of mythologized, concrete images. Not only are "troubles"
put into the context of a force of nature, in the "sea of
troubles," but the difficulties which beset Hamlet are treated
in terms of a quasi personification: "the slings and arrows of
outrageous fortune." What Shakespeare has done is to adapt
to his own purposes an image based upon the mythological
goddess Fortuna, so as to express the human problem in the

face of which Hamlet stands perplexed and almost over-
whelmed. If this mythological usage were merely ornamental,
it might be "demythologized," but the "slings and arrows of
outrageous fortune" and the taking "arms against a sea
of troubles" do not constitute decorations which may be
stripped away, leaving the basic idea bare for all to see. These
images *are* the idea, they do not merely adorn it; the figures
used are not figures of speech, but are rather figures of
thought.

Without attempting to exhaust the meaning of those figures, let me suggest the direction in which they are moved
by the thought which is inherent in them. Hamlet, in facing
the universal human problem of evil, is virtually immobilized
by the choice which he must make: to endure passively or
resist actively. The enormity of the problem for a sensitive
spirit comes out again and again in Hamlet's speeches, which
are relevant not only for his own situation but for that of
any man who is faced with the core problems of human existence. Evil, injustice, hatred, all are tangible enough when
Hamlet speaks of suffering them as slings and arrows; but
when it comes to opposing them, to taking arms against them,
they seem to take on a different shape, the shape of the sea,
unassailable by any human effort. Thus we have the utter
aptness of the very tangible slings and arrows of a very tangible fortune tormenting Hamlet, and in the next breath the
evanescent and elusive sea of troubles against which he may
take up only ineffective arms. His dilemma is thus posed so
cogently by these imagistic figures of thought that with them
he moves along in his consideration of suicide as a possible
means of escape from what appears an impossible situation.
This, or something rather like it, is what Hamlet is thinking. Yet even if we agree upon this interpretation as basically
sound, we must also see, if we understand the passage at all,
that Hamlet's soliloquy cannot be reduced to categories other

than its own. The literary use of metaphor and parable is a
highly skilled specialization of ordinary speech, which can be
just as careful and coherent as that of science or of existential
philosophy. Literary metaphors, as such, are not concerned
with the creation of exact replicas of anything, but rather
with bringing living realities to mind.

This is so even for so tangible a reality as war, for as
Tolstoi says, "in every description of a battle there is a necessary lie, resulting from the need of describing in a few words
the actions of thousands of men spread over several miles."[47]
The "necessary lie" which is an integral part of every type of
literature which we have noted so far is also a part of the great
literary-philosophical dialogues of Plato, who frequently con-
structs "myths" of the afterlife, or of the soul wandering
through the regions of the beyond, or mounting on wings to
God. Plato concentrated not on demythologizing thought, but
rather upon mythologizing it, because in this fashion he
could, as he said, "render falsehood useful to us, as the closest
attainable copy of the truth."[48]

Plato clearly regarded the myth-making process as the most
practicable method of dealing with the nature of man, the
nature of God, and the nature of the relationships between
man and God, here and hereafter. Benjamin Jowett summed
up the method when he wrote that for Plato

> the mythus is not a mere garment, thrown over a thought that
> had previously existed in a purely scientific shape; in many
> cases it is for Plato a positive necessity, and his masterly use
> of it is a consequence of the fact that he does not turn back
> upon the path of reflection to seek a picture for his thought,
> but that from the very outset, like a creative artist, *he thinks
> in pictures.*[49]

Whenever, as for Plato, the "mythus is not a mere garment,
thrown over a thought," but in a basic sense *is* the thought,

for "he thinks in pictures," then it is impossible to get behind the myth and to translate it either onto a literal or onto an abstract plane without destroying its thought and substituting another thought for it. While it may be possible either by literalizing or by demythologizing to make something clear to a modern man, what is made clear is fundamentally different from what was there in the first place. And this will be true regardless of whether modern man finds acceptable either what was originally there or what is substituted for it.

We have now explored with some care the relevance for Christian theology, first of the techniques of dramatic history, and then of the three related principles of accommodation, of the willing suspension of disbelief, and of the distinctive validity of literary truth. Throughout, of course, I have attempted to state the case for a literary approach to truth, as this approach may contribute to the integrity, depth, and vigor of Christian thought—or, as Martin Luther put it, to "pure theology." At this point literary insights are indispensable for, as Luther proceeded to say, it is by literary study "as by no other means, [that] people are wonderfully fitted for the grasping of sacred truth and for handling it skillfully and happily."[50] Luther's admonition represents the general assumption underlying these essays. As for this particular chapter, it may be most appropriately concluded by referring to the advice which John Bunyan gave to the readers of *Pilgrim's Progress:*

> Take heed also that thou be not extreme
> In playing with the *outside* of my dream;
> Nor let my figure or similitude
> Put thee into a laughter or a feud.
> Leave this for *boys* and *fools;* but as for thee,
> Do thou the substance of my matter see.[51]

PART II

*The Literature
of Clarification*

Chapter Two

LITERATURE AND
THE GREATNESS OF MAN

I. *The Clarification of Life*

Man is inescapably engaged in the evaluation of his life and of the alternatives which his life presents to him. Apart from evaluation he cannot live, for life consists of a series of choices apart from which action is impossible. He may, of course, choose superficially, or naïvely, or unwisely, but choose he must and every choice has at its base an evaluation. By literature man may be assisted in relating his evaluations to the general conditions of human existence in terms of beauty, understanding, and compassion. In this way literature both undergirds and increases the greatness of man.

Sir Philip Sidney followed and summarized the perennial classical view of literature when he defined poetry as "an art of imitation . . . with this end, to teach and delight."[1] In our own time Robert Frost puts it in a slightly different way, but to the same purpose when he writes that poetry "begins in delight and ends in wisdom," or in "a clarification of life." This literary clarification may be a small one, but nonetheless valuable, such as we can so often find in the poetry of Frost himself, or it may be a great clarification such as is found in the writings of Shakespeare and Sophocles, or it may even be an ultimate clarification, such as is found in the Christian Scriptures, but genuine literature always offers some new and clearer vision of reality. This is its greatest value to the generality of men, for as Frost says, "we are always hurling experience ahead of us to pave the future with against the day when we may want to strike a line of purpose across it for somewhere."[2]

This much is so even when the writer is focusing our attention upon inanimate nature, for the result here as elsewhere must be a clarification of life. As Walt Whitman put it, people "expect of the poet to indicate more than the beauty and dignity which always attach to dumb real objects —they expect him to indicate the path between reality and their souls."[3] Literature, then, even when it is regarded as a mirror held up to nature, is a mirror with a difference; it is not a mere replica reproduction of something external and objective. George Bernard Shaw described the mirror of art in this way: "You use a glass mirror to see your face; you use works of art to see your soul."[4]

The result is not just the expression of the writer's individualistic view, but is the communication of something relevant to the entire human situation. "The efforts of the best poets and esthetic writers," Goethe wrote, "have been directed toward the universally human."[5] William Faulkner made the same point when he declared that all genuine writers belong to one universal school of man, treating in a mutual language "much older than any intellectual tongue because it is the simple language of humanity," "a very old story . . . the story of human beings in conflict with their nature, their character, their souls, with others, or with their environment."[6]

The clarification of life, a deeper understanding of the human situation, the charting of pathways between reality and the human soul, the treatment of the universally human in the simple language of humanity—these are characteristics of great literature. So understood, literature provides insights into the human situation which we ignore only to our peril and to the foreshortening of our understanding. In this sense Abelard raised a very foolish question when he asked: "What has Horace to do with the Psalter, Virgil with the Gospel, Cicero with the Apostle?"[7] The answer is simply that Horace, Virgil, and Cicero clarify the human situation to which the salvation of God is addressed through Psalter, Gospel, and Apostle. Christianity cannot deny the value of Horace, Virgil, and Cicero without denying the value of man, which it cannot do and remain Christian. Concerned as it is with man in his greatness and his misery, Christian faith addresses itself to the very situation which literature clarifies, examines, and makes in some limited measure manageable.

And yet the question of relevance has been repeatedly raised, whether with Abelard as we have seen, or with Tertullian's "What has Athens to do with Jerusalem," or Alcuin's "What has Ingeld to do with Christ," or Erasmus' "What has Aristotle to do with Christ." A highly intelligent answer to these questions was proposed some four centuries ago by John Calvin. Now Calvin was surely not one to overestimate man apart from the grace of God, but neither was he willing to underestimate him. Of the value of secular, and even pagan, literature, Calvin wrote:

> So oft therefore as we light upon profane writers, let us be put in mind by that marvelous light of truth that shineth in them, that the mind of man, how much so ever it be perverted and fallen from the first integrity, is yet still clothed and garnished with excellent gifts of God. If we consider that the spirit of God is the only fountain of truth, we will neither refuse nor despise the truth itself, wheresoever it shall appear, except we will dishonorably use the Spirit of God: for the gifts of the Holy Ghost cannot be set light by, without contempt and reproach of Himself.[8]

It is indisputable, of course, that great literature not only may serve but often has served as a bearer of Christian truth, as in the works of Dante and Milton, for example, and later chapters will deal with such works. For the present, however, we are concerned with literature as bearing general human truth, as we have seen this understood by Goethe, Faulkner, and Calvin, among others. Let us return now to Faulkner and his statement that literature concerns "the old universal truths" of human anguish and triumph. "All writers," Faulkner says, "deal in the same truth because there's [sic] not very many different phases of it."[9] These old universal truths Mr. C. S. Lewis in his *Abolition of Man* calls the *Tao*, the conception of human values, of character, understanding, pity, honor, and virtue which run through all the lasting forms of humane thought, "Platonic, Aristotelian, Stoic, Christian and Oriental alike."[10] There can be no living of man together with man in any civilized way apart from these ancient values, for apart from them there never has been and never can be any civilization. They are the *given* upon which all human value and humane life rests, the *Tao* or way upon which all men and societies must walk if any human dignity and worth is to be maintained. Lewis, as a Christian, knows that the *Tao* is not the equivalent of Christian faith and cannot be substituted for it, but he is also, like Calvin, too profound and too literate a Christian thinker ever to assume that these universal truths can be ignored by Christians "except we will dishonorably use the Spirit of God."[11]

This universal truth to the human situation, this *Tao*, may be memorably treated by men who are in their own lives mean, little, and even wicked. Two eminent Christian writers, Milton and Tolstoi, both held that the poet must be a good man, and their opinion is sometimes falsely taken to be the Christian position. It is not. Augustine wrote that, in order that God's good gift of beauty not be made an idol, "God dispenses it even to the wicked,"[12] while Thomas Aquinas held that "the test of the artist does not lie in the will with which he goes to work, but in the excellence of the work he produces."[13] John Calvin elaborated the same position when he discussed the attribution in Genesis of arts and skills to the wicked line of Cain, through Jabal, Jubal, and Tubal-cain. "The invention of arts and such other like things which serve for the common use and benefit of life," Calvin wrote, "is the gift of God, not to be despised, and a virtue worthy to be praised," despite the fact that "the same people which had most swerved from all integrity, excelled all the rest of Adam's posterity in gifts not to be repented of."[14] Calvin thus interpreted the development of the arts among Cain's descendants as an indication that although they were without grace they were not without all good, but were through art showing "the beams of God's glory" in praiseworthy ways.[15] The point, then, is that the three leading theologians of the Christian tradition—Augustine, Aquinas, and Calvin—unite with non-Christian critics in assuring us that we are not to judge the value of a literary work by the life of its author. The common caricature of the poet as an amoral eccentric, a caricature which is so popularly accepted in our time, is decidedly unfair to most *great* poets, but even where it applies it does not invalidate works of literature which carry value in their own right, quite apart from the lives of the men who produced them.

II. *The Failure of Glandular Writing*

We have thus far been considering literature which we might call good or great, whose function is to teach and delight: literature which begins in delight and ends in the clarification of life, in the holding up of a mirror to the human soul. Such literature differs from what may be called vulgate fiction, of the potboiler variety, in that vulgate writing rarely gets beyond entertainment, beyond the provision of a lift or a thrill, an escape from life's problems or a basking in the projections of wish-fulfillment, such as is provided in the adventures of Tarzan or Superman. In such writing we evade anxiety through fun, with the reiterated reassurance that all will eventually be well for the fortunate people with whom the reader identifies himself in some magic never-never land. Or there is, on a slightly less appealing level, the soap-opera type of fiction in which the housewife finds mirrored an endless succession of problems which may add interest to her own life and before which her own problems may seem small. The result again is a diversion from life rather than a full and meaningful encounter with it.

Then there are those forms of popular fiction which furnish the ersatz excitements of sex or sadism, heady dishes of a quite sensationalist approach. Beatings, maulings, murders, and rapes put on by subhuman men and women—not to mention monsters from the deep and creatures from a Martian lagoon —whip up an increasingly frenzied taste for violence and sensation. And when physical violence is absent, there is the ever-present emphasis on sex. Time and time again the reading public consumes the fictional notion that sex is an ultimate end in itself, and that men and women are objects for the gratification of sexual urges. Charles Williams describes a woman who may stand as typical of a certain sort of modern heroine: "She had the common, vague idea of her age that if your sexual life was all right, you were all right, and she had the common vague idea of all ages that if you (and your sexual life) were not all right, it was probably someone else's fault."[16] We are reminded of *The New Yorker* cartoon of a delighted publisher who holds in his hands the manuscript of a novel while he praises the author by saying, in effect,

"Your action moves swiftly, your characters are well developed, and what's more, you have a very dirty mind."

Such sensationalism does not get at what we mean by significant human truths. William Faulkner has summarized for us the efforts of such a sensationalist author:

> He labors under a curse. He writes not of love but of lust, of defeats in which nobody loses anything of value, of victories without hope and, worst of all, without pity or compassion. His griefs grieve on no universal bones, leaving no scars. He writes not of the heart but of the glands.[17]

Such glandular literature falls far short of greatness, but this falling short does not come as a result of the use of evil, but as a result of the use of "evil for the sake of the evil," rather than "to show man's soul in conflict with his evil nature or his environment," as Faulkner puts it.[18] To be sure, great literature must treat evil, sometimes in a base and repulsive form, even as Faulkner himself repeatedly does, and indeed as do the Christian Scriptures and much great poetry everywhere. Thus, to take one example, Dante had to pass through hell as a necessary stage of his journey to heaven, but he never settled down there to contemplate iniquity as an end in itself. Only the damned did that, and yet that is what a certain amount of contemporary glandular writing invites its readers to do.

The result is what Prof. Gilbert Highet, of Columbia University, refers to as the creation of an unhealthy and unreal dream world. Of the mass-produced glandular fiction of our age, Mr. Highet writes:

> The growth of immorality, especially among young men and girls, and in particular of deliberate cruelty, drunkenness, and sexual promiscuity [are] vices which are not merely condoned, but actually praised and enjoyed by the most admired characters in these assembly-line books and magazines. It frankly re-

volts me to know that the only American writer whose books have sold over ten million copies is Mickey Spillane. You may say that Mr. Spillane is not a cause, but a symptom; yet I think I should disagree. Everyone who writes bears the responsibility for presenting a social picture and a set of moral beliefs to his readers; the simpler and stupider his readers are, the more receptive they will be, and the greater his responsibility; and very few modern authors can ever have offered a more debased and debasing picture of the world to their readers—or shall we say their victims?

Even in the more ambitious and purportedly more serious works of such writers as Jack Kerouac and James Jones, Mr. Highet continues, the fictional characters "inhabit a world just a step or two above the gat-and-moll-and-spiked-knucks world of Mr. Spillane. Cultivated people have always been in a minority. But is this the first time in history when they have been made to feel ashamed of it?"[19] The primary objection to glandular fiction, then, is simply that it belittles man.

While I could scarcely agree more heartily than I do with Mr. Highet's basic appraisal of the sex and sadism school of fiction, one further thing should be said about it. There is an unconscious revelation even here, rudimentary and unformed though it may be. Man's restless and relentless search for escape through passion and violence still shows something. For the reader and writer of merely glandular fiction there seems to be some implied necessity to seek sexual satisfaction on the printed page, as though they were incompetent to find it in mutual human relationships in marriage, and also to find in the violence of bloodletting and the thrill of power some compensation for the smallness and fearfulness of their lives as men—and perhaps emotionally unbalanced men, at that. Thus the vast craze for brutal murder mysteries underscores the fact that every man regards himself on the unconscious level as a murderer—"we know that deep down in our hearts we are all murderers," psychiatrist Martin Grotjahn writes—while in another sense we may identify ourselves "with the detective or even with the victim who was murdered."[20] Thus we may indulge ourselves, at the same time, on one level with the age-old sin of Cain, and on another level with a rigoristic and self-righteous legalism. Or turn to the fiction of dread and suspense which displays, albeit crudely, man's ultimate terror in the face of the horrors which come upon him, even though they may at least in part arise out of him, as we see objectified on the movie screen a monster rising out of the deep to threaten men, or a mad scientist rising out of the laboratory to unleash a horror upon men, or even, as in *The Night of the Hunter,* a mad clergyman riding through the night, singing "Leaning on the Everlasting Arms" as he seeks the death of two "lambs" of his flock. Out of it all comes an image of man at the end of his rope, or, if you will, at the end of his halter, trembling on the abyss of some terrifying and ultimate personal disaster. And that, crudely represented, is the state of man in nature, without God. It may not be a truth which is intended by the glandular writers, and it is stumblingly set forth, but it is nonetheless there for those who have eyes to see it and ears to hear it.

III. *The Major Concerns: Beauty, Understanding, and Compassion*

But such a mirror as glandular fiction holds up to life is at best broken, clouded, and distorting. It is different in the literary masterworks, to which men return generation after generation in search of a more profound clarification of the human situation. Here we find the full gamut of man—man in his greatness and his misery, in his almost limitless potential and in his equally limitless frustration, "the glory, jest, and riddle of the world," as Alexander Pope called him.[21] And from such literature, I would like to suggest, we can gain sustenance for our own basic humanity through the nurture of beauty, the nurture of understanding, and the nurture of compassion. In each of these ways literature both points toward and contributes to human greatness.

First, there is the nurture of beauty. We go far astray if we regard beauty as mere ornament or decoration, as a filigree attached to the surface of life. Yet it is too often regarded in this way, and in America especially the general appreciation of beauty is on a very low plane indeed. Walk into a typical American house and you find all the utility which credit can afford, but an appalling poverty of beauty. When you do find a few individual objects of some beauty they too often fail to harmonize either with each other or with the rest of the room in which they are placed. This pervasive Philistinism of American taste is sometimes rather glibly attributed to our Puritan heritage, but the attribution is false, as you can readily discover if you study the planning, architecture, and interiors of New England villages. One of the most striking ironies in the history of taste is that the creators of the lovely Puritan houses, village greens, and churches should be called tasteless by twentieth-century men who are themselves submerged in the most appalling mass of ugliness and vulgarity which the Western world has perhaps ever known.

In our culture it is difficult to develop a sense of taste in a natural way, as a normal matter of course. Instead we appoint for ourselves various commissioners of taste, such as interior decorators and art critics, and we expect them to look after beauty. But to expect beauty to be cared for in this way is, again, to treat it as mere ornamentation, a frill which we may wish to add to our lives. Beauty will not be well served in this way, and neither will the commissars of beauty. When society as a whole is insensitive to beauty, then the cultivation of beauty too often becomes the specialized cultivation of a hot-house plant and is regarded either as a hobby or as a cult. In these circumstances, the cultivator himself runs the risk of becoming a dilettante or a fanatic, and there is not much to commend either alternative. In the meanwhile the inattention to beauty shuts off society at large from one of the major sources of its spiritual sustenance.

Beauty is not excrescent to the general well-being of man, but essential to it. Beauty brings order out of anarchy, harmony out of cacophony. Beauty, at base, is the result of the creative activity of God, and artistic beauty is, if I may strain the terms, a humanly created revelation. Thus Shelley declared of poetry that it "lifts the veil from the hidden beauty of the world."[22] Art reveals beauty to us, makes us conscious of what we ignore. When we read in *Hamlet* that "the morn, in russet mantle clad, Walks o'er the dew of yon high eastward hill,"[23] we have had a veil lifted from the world's hidden beauty and we see that beauty afresh both *in* Shakespeare's words and *through* those words.

To paraphrase Coleridge we may say that the sense of beauty consists in the intuition of the proportioned relations of parts to each other and to a whole, the melody of the parts being united in the harmony of the whole.[24] Beauty comes to us as we perceive an ordered and harmoniously proportioned creation. Thus understood, beauty involves the fusion of free life and confining form. That is what Christopher Fry has called the logic of beauty, and of it he says: "What part this logic plays in our life here on earth is beyond calculation. If it awakens harmony, modulation, and the resolving of discord in us, we are nearer to our true natures."[25] When beauty is understood in that sense—and it has been so understood by the great Christian humanists—it becomes clear why beauty is an essential to the health of individuals and of societies.

Art must thus be seen as indispensable to human well-being, and beauty is very closely allied to goodness. But beauty is *not* goodness. As Coleridge puts it, "the beautiful is thus at once distinguished both from the *agreeable,* which is beneath it, and from the *good,* which is above it: for both these have an interest necessarily attached to them: both act on the *will,* and excite a desire for the actual existence of the image or idea contemplated: while the sense of beauty rests gratified in the mere contemplation or intuition."[26] In this regard beauty is comparable to courage, in that both are neutral values which may be applied toward the ends of evil as well as the ends of goodness. Aldous Huxley has recently made this point with great force, by considering the "beauties of unholiness" as well as the "beauties of holiness." He writes that the

"beauties of holiness" strengthen faith where it already exists and, where there is no faith, contribute to conversion. Appealing, as they do, only to the aesthetic sense, they guarantee neither the truth nor the ethical value of the doctrines with which they have been, quite arbitrarily, associated. As a matter of plain historical fact, the beauties of holiness have often been matched and indeed surpassed by the beauties of unholiness. Under Hitler, for example, the yearly Nuremberg rallies were masterpieces of ritual and theatrical art. "I had spent six years in St. Petersburg before the war in the best days of the old Russian ballet," writes Sir Nevile Henderson, the British ambassador to Hitler's Germany, "but for grandiose beauty I have never seen any ballet to compare with the Nuremberg rally." One thinks of Keats—"beauty is truth, truth beauty." Alas, the identity exists only on some ultimate, supramundane level. On the levels of politics and theology, beauty is perfectly compatible with nonsense and tyranny.[27]

The point which Mr. Huxley makes is a very important one indeed, and should be kept in mind in any discussion of beauty. Basically, however, the function of beauty when it expresses itself without perversion to false goals is to nurture a higher and more harmonious life for man.

In addition to the nurture of beauty, literature also provides for the nurture of understanding, a broadening of horizons and a deepening of awareness, which may come in many ways. It may come through a brief phrase which clarifies for us some particular human personality, or even in a seemingly chance witticism which illuminates the entire human landscape, like a momentary flash in the darkness. I know of no contemporary writer more adept in this way than Mr. Peter de Vries. What brings us closer, in a single phrase, to an understanding of man's pompous helplessness than de Vries' description of the "man who could dive but not swim"? That phrase could almost stand as a poetic definition of what theology means by the state of sin, and so too could Mr. de Vries' remark about a sophisticate with the reputation for profundity that he is profound "only on the surface. Down deep, he's shallow." And we may find an emblem for our entire contemporary culture in his description of a couple who loved to drive a convertible through New York in the dead of winter "with the top down and the heater turned on."[28] Each phrase cuts to the core of the human situation, strips away the various disguises and poses behind which man seeks to hide his own ultimate inadequacies. Or again, in a far less gifted writer than Peter de Vries, we find that Mr. George Axelrod in his *Will Success Spoil Rock Hunter?* describes someone who combines the apparent confidence and actual panic of a man who suddenly finds himself on the upper levels of success.[29]

Beyond the limited attainments of Axelrod and the impressive performance of de Vries, however, we find a most marked increase of human understanding available to us in the writings of William Shakespeare. Let us look particularly

at his *Antony and Cleopatra* where the tragedy focuses upon
the effects of infatuation upon a great and noble man. The
entire frivolity of a pampered life, centered upon indulgence
and amusement, suddenly flashes upon us in the phrase of
Cleopatra's lady in waiting, Charmian, when she drawls out,
"I love long life better than figs."[30] Here the total but not
entirely unappealing decadence of Oriental ease and self-
indulgence is set off in a phrase against the classic Roman
ideal of Stoic fortitude and adherence to duty. In Shakespeare's *Antony and Cleopatra* the tragedy of Antony rests in
his vacillation between these two attitudes, and in his final
rejection of the Roman virtues. Antony knows what is at
stake and early in the play recognizes that he must tear himself away from his devoted slavery to Cleopatra:

> These strong Egyptian fetters I must break
> Or lose myself in dotage.[31]

Again, at a later point, he declares that "If I lose mine honor,
I lose myself."[32] Yet he willfully throws away his "absolute
soldiership," gradually loosens his hold upon the empire for
love of Cleopatra, and eventually becomes "the noble ruin
of her magic."[33] The entire action is at base undisciplined
and certainly un-Roman, as Antony both knows and acknowledges, so that Antony's tragedy is not so much the loss
of empire as it is the loss of his own established identity.
Despite his frenzied cries toward the end, in the catastrophe
which he has knowingly brought upon himself, that "I am
Antony yet,"[34] those who know him best repeatedly bewail
his repudiation of his own nature under the charm of Cleopatra, a charm which he follows to his own destruction.

And yet there is a nobleness even in this man's fall, a nobleness and an appealing quality which make it impossible for
us to repudiate Antony as a mere libertine. Knowing Cleopatra as Shakespeare presents her—

> Age cannot wither nor custom stale
> Her infinite variety. Other women cloy
> The appetites they feed, but she makes hungry
> Where most she satisfies; for vilest things
> Become themselves in her, that the holy priests
> Bless her when she is riggish[35]—

we understand the fatal attraction which can seize upon the life of a strong man and destroy him. "There but for the grace of God go I," we might say, or, with the doctor who discovers the secret of Lady Macbeth's murderous dreams, "God, God forgive us all." Shakespeare does not oversimplify things for us, or fit them into the compass of small minds. Instead, he expands our understanding toward a fuller comprehension. He never approves Antony's license and self-indulgence at the expense of the peace and stability of the civilized world, but he does lead us to understand what can happen to a man caught up in the strong toil of some infatuating grace. We repudiate the choice, but not the man who made it, as even Augustus Caesar cried "poor Antony" and weeps the death of the man who chose to be his enemy.[36] "His taints and honours Wag'd equal with him," Maecenas says, and we agree.[37]

Having destroyed his life, Antony cannot even successfully consummate his own suicide, but thrusts his sword wrongly, and so lingers on to die in the arms of the queen whose love he earlier chose despite his certainty that from this choice would follow "ten thousand harms more than the ills I know."[38] Although he had "given his empire Up to a whore,"[39] as Caesar thought, Antony dies in a love which cannot be dismissed or disdained:

> I am dying, Egypt, dying; only
> I here importune death awhile, until
> Of many thousand kisses the poor last
> I lay upon thy lips.[40]

Darkness covers the end of all, but it is a darkness of human dignity. "Our strength is all gone into heaviness," says Cleopatra, and her lady in waiting declares, "The bright day is done, And we are for the dark."[41] The world which valued life in terms of figs comes to its inevitable end in the basket of figs which contains the poisonous asp by which Cleopatra chose to die.

Antony and Cleopatra does not lead us to the repudiation of order and peace and social coherence in favor of individual infatuation, and Shakespeare certainly did not intend that it should do so. But neither did he intend, nor do we feel, a self-righteous repudiation of the characters involved, a pharisaic passing by on the other side. What we feel, on the contrary, is an increased awareness of the beauty and fragility, the greatness and tragedy of human existence as it comes before us in this play. We leave the play with a profound increment of understanding for the man who is caught up in the enticements of life and destroyed in the tensions between love and duty. And we know how it happened.

So it is that the increment of understanding may bring with it an increment of compassion. But this process is not the same as that which is summarized in the proverbial statement that to understand all is to forgive all, a proverb which George Bernard Shaw calls "the Devil's sentimentality."[42] We do not conclude the sin to be no sin; we rather understand, and have compassion for, the intensely human sinner caught up in the fetters of a sin which might also be our own, a sin which destroys the sinner but which still does not totally consume his human dignity. Antony is still our brother, and might be ourselves. But when all the rudiments of humanity are absent, on the other hand, compassion becomes impossible even though understanding may still be present. Thus we understand the sensual Antony with compassion, but in another treatment involving sensuality, Aldous

Huxley's *Brave New World,* the understanding is such as to make compassion impossible.

In this novel Huxley writes almost apocalyptically of a society so totally controlled that even the most basic humanity is obliterated. Projecting his action into the future as a prophetic warning to the present, Huxley describes a world state in which all personal conduct and thought and economics and science are rigidly stereotyped, and all persons produced by a sort of bottling plant assembly line to meet the demands of an impersonal and dehumanizing state. Conduct is so automated, and life so formalized, that no opportunity is afforded for thought or suffering or solitude. Here we find the ultimate consummation of the "organization man" mentality which even in our own time threatens to engulf and destroy the integrity of the individual. The whole meticulous standardization of what Huxley has ironically called a brave new world is directed toward preventing anyone from feeling, even for a short time, any individuation or any want which goes unsatisfied. "Everyone belongs to everyone else" is a formula which all are conditioned from childhood to accept, and which finds its ultimate expression in the socially imposed obligation to be promiscuous, so that any departure from the standard of strict promiscuity is treated as shameful. And then there is soma, a drug representing the development of the cocktail into an opiate with no painful aftereffects, in which it is socially shameful not to indulge. By means of soma one may wrap oneself in a cozy protection against the infringement of any unpleasantness, especially the unpleasantness of thought. The result is that people become machines, automata given over to incessant and unremitting self-gratification, isolated from any possibility of genuine religion or science or beauty, in a world where original investigation and discovery of new truth are outlawed and the old perennial truths of man are proscribed. Thus the Bible and

Shakespeare are both classed as "pornography" in a society which regards lust and indulgence as virtue.

There are a few, to be sure, who escape from this synthetic perversion of Utopia, but apart from these we feel no sympathy for the impersonal figures who populate *Brave New World*, scampering from soma to soma, from diversion to diversion, "from girl to pneumatic girl." Indeed, Huxley would have us feel no sympathy, but shock and revulsion. We can understand Marc Antony and accept him in compassion, but for Huxley's characters we can only feel what his hero feels, "an intense overpowering hatred of these less than human monsters."[43]

So it is that in Huxley's novel we are caught up into a new understanding of human life through the portrayal of the negation of human values, as our attention is startlingly focused upon the old sins and new conformities within our own society which threaten to reduce us to the less than human monsters we find in *Brave New World*. *That* we can understand, and desperately need to understand, but by very virtue of our understanding of the processes by which man is dehumanized we can feel no compassion for the processes as such or for the automated life which results from them.

The nurture of compassion thus comes only through the focus upon a common humanity. Shut up as most of us are within the narrow compass of our own lives, we do not naturally break out from ourselves either into the larger world which surrounds us or into the other small worlds of individuals whose lives impinge upon our own. Although it is true that man cannot ultimately and finally free himself from bondage to himself by his own efforts—as there is a sort of law of psychodynamics operating here according to which we cannot lift ourselves by our own bootstraps—it is equally true that there may be some proximate breaking down of barriers between man and man. Upon this proximate and limited break-through of man to meet man all worthy human society is based, and to it art contributes by the enlargement of understanding but even more by the expansion of sympathy. This is what Tolstoi meant when he wrote that "art should cause violence to be set aside,"[44] and Shelley got at it even more explicitly when he wrote that literature provides, through the imagination, the means by which one man may put himself in the place of other men:

> The great secret of morals is love, or a going out of our nature, and an identification of ourselves with the beautiful which exists in thought, action or person, not our own. A man, to be greatly good, must imagine intensely and comprehensively; he must put himself in the place of another and of many others; the pains and pleasures of his species must become his own. The great instrument of moral good is the imagination; and poetry administers to the effect by acting upon the cause.[45]

This nurture of compassion by means of the imaginative identification of literature may be seen in many forms. A few years ago there was on Broadway a perceptive play by John Osborne called *The Entertainer,* a play which portrayed the life of a seedy, vulgar, and revolting British vaudeville comedian named Archie. Sir Laurence Olivier acted the title role, and the result was a remarkable performance by means of which we could enter into empathy with a type of man whom most of us would never know in any other way, and from whom in real life we would in all likelihood turn away in revulsion. And to justify such a turning away we could point to Archie's utter disregard of persons other than himself, his attempted abandonment of his wife, his virtual blackmail of a brother, and his total humiliation of his aged father. But seeing Archie as we did through Osborne's words and Olivier's portrayal we could understand and sympathize with this undeniably small and self-centered man for whom life seemed to have no real dignity and no real joy, and who attempted to compensate for the drab meaninglessness which he found in his own existence by drink, adultery, and the cheap and hackneyed performances he put on before British music house audiences. And thus a man for whom we can feel no possible admiration takes on significance as a human being so trapped within himself that his major efforts at self-assertion are the throwing of bawdy burlesque jokes into the face of what he feels to be a meaningless and perhaps even hostile universe. In this poor strutting player we find something universally significant for the natural condition of man, and in ourselves a deepening of consciousness and of compassion.

The same result, as we would expect, is far more profoundly effected by William Shakespeare. Surely the most compassionate play in English literature is *King Lear,* where we see what Shelley called the intense and comprehensive imagination employed to put us in empathy with some of the most basic pains of human life. What could be more moving than Lear's words to the ungrateful daughter who turns him out of her house:

> I prithee, daughter, do not make me mad.
> I would not trouble thee, my child; farewell.
> We'll no more meet, no more see one another.
> But yet thou art my flesh, my blood, my daughter. . . .[46]

Or again:

> How sharper than a serpent's tooth it is
> To have a thankless child![47]

Or this speech which Lear makes when he is deprived of all his attendant knights on the grounds that as an old and abdicated king he "needs" no attendants:

> O, reason not the need! Our basest beggars
> Are in the poorest things superfluous.
> Allow not nature more than nature needs,
> Man's life is cheap as beast's.[48]

And so the old and superannuated protests against being reduced to a state of no value and of no dignity. Nowhere can the young better learn to understand what this means than in *King Lear*.

But Lear does not merely suffer: he grows through his suffering, takes on added human dignity by bearing the indignities which are heaped upon him. The theme of growth through suffering is universal to man. The chorus to Sophocles' *Antigone* puts it that "for mortals greatly to live is greatly to suffer,"[49] and Euripides has the old Trojan Queen Hecuba, sitting before the ruins of her destroyed city, declare that "had not God turned us in his hand and cast to earth our greatness, we would have passed away giving nothing to men. They would have found no theme for song in us nor made great poems from our sorrows."[50] Although the theme of growth toward human greatness through suffering may be universal, it is fortunate for Lear that no Job's comforter comes to cheer him with it. He learns it for himself and on his own. Thus at the very lowest pitch of extremity as he wanders in rags, a fugitive in the country which he had once ruled, he can say of himself with new truth that he is "every inch a king."[51] And Shakespeare never tells us that we should feel compassion for Lear, but rather leads us to feel it, just as he leads Lear himself to feel compassion for others:

> Poor naked wretches, wheresoe'er you are,
> That bide the pelting of this pitiless storm,
> How shall your houseless heads and unfed sides,
> Your loop'd and window'd raggedness, defend you
> From seasons such as these? O, I have ta'en
> Too little care of this! Take physic, pomp;
> Expose thyself to feel what wretches feel,
> That thou mayst shake the superflux to them
> And show the heavens more just.[52]

If ever an age needed compassion it is our own age, and yet the very brutality of our era seems to inoculate us against compassion, for we do not hear of murders and persecutions of single men and women but of mass slaughter, of the deportation and oppression of thousands and even millions. The numbers are so staggering that we soon lose a sense of proportion and hide ourselves from human suffering by a barrier of statistics. But literature breaks through that barrier for us, and brings us into feeling relationship with all human suffering by exposing us to it in critical instances. One such instance was the fall of Troy, which has ever since served Western man for insight into human suffering, and which the Greek dramatist Euripides used as the setting for his tragedy, *The Trojan Women*. In that drama, Troy has already been captured by the Greeks, and its defenders slain. All that is left is a band of captive women about to be carried into slavery—the ancient equivalent of our displaced persons. The princess Andromache sits on the beach awaiting deportation. Her husband, Hector, the greatest and noblest Trojan of whom it was said that "only Hector guarded Ilios," had long since been killed outside the walls of his city. As Andromache sits waiting, holding in her arms her small son Astyanax, an enemy soldier tells her of the Greek decision to kill the boy by casting him from the highest tower of the city, lest he grow to a manhood like that of his father Hector and avenge himself upon the conquerors. At this tragic moment Andromache speaks to her child in a way which universalizes her pain and brings us into a feeling relationship with it:

> Go, die, my best-beloved, my cherished one,
> In fierce men's hands, leaving me here alone.
> . . . Weepest thou?
> Nay, why, my little one? Thou canst not know.
> And Father will not come; he will not come;
> Not once, the great spear flashing, and the tomb
> Riven to set thee free!
> How shall it be? One horrible spring . . . deep, deep
> Down. And thy neck . . . Ah God, so cometh sleep? . . .
> And none to pity thee! Thou little thing

That curlest in my arms, what sweet scents cling
All round thy neck! Belovéd: can it be
All nothing, that this bosom cradled thee
And fostered; all the weary nights, wherethrough
I watched upon thy sickness, till I grew
Wasted with watching? Kiss me. This one time;
Not ever again. Put up thine arms and climb
About my neck: now, kiss me, lips to lips . . .
Quick! take him: drag him: cast him from the wall,
If cast ye will! Tear him, ye beasts, be swift!
God hath undone me, and I cannot lift
One hand, one hand, to save my child from death.[53]

If the beauty and the pathos of that ancient Greek passage ever really penetrates our consciousness, it will not be so easy again to pass over the miseries of the dispossessed in our own time: at least some of the proximate barriers which separate man from man will have been broken down, and we will have been enfranchised to a larger awareness of the value implicit in every human life.

Literature, then, serves to deepen and to extend human greatness through the nurture of beauty, understanding, and compassion. In none of these ways, of course, can literature, unless it be the literature of Christian faith, lead us to the City of God, but it may make our life in the city of man far more a thing of joy and meaning and humanity, and that in itself is no small achievement. Great literature may not be a Jacob's ladder by which we can climb to heaven, but it provides an invaluable staff with which to walk the earth.

IV. *The Ultimate Questions*

But there are also points at which wisdom comes to an end, times when suffering seems meaningless and places where insight seems only to stare into an inscrutable void. At such times and places we, like Sophocles' Creon, "stand once more on the edge of fate,"[54] or we share the haunting, mystic, vague, unhappy, nameless loneliness of Euripides: "Whatever far-off state there may be that is dearer to man than life, Darkness has it in her arms and hides it in cloud. We are love-sick for this namless thing that glitters here on the earth, because no man has tasted another life, because the things under us are unrevealed, and we float upon a stream of legend."[55] We thus come upon that doubt and uncertainty and tentativeness with which the honest natural man looks out upon the ultimate relationships of his existence, as man's misery overtakes his greatness and the limits of human vision run out, and he finds himself, as Alexander Pope put it, "In doubt to deem himself a god, or beast, In doubt his mind or body to prefer; Born but to die, and reas'ning but to err."[56]

At this point man, "the glory, jest, and riddle of the world," cannot solve his own ultimate riddle, but can only pose it. At best he can see the questions which his existence finally involves, can raise and clarify these questions, but he cannot solve them. His greatness now rests, as Pascal put it, in the recognition of his own misery.[57] It is to this recognition of man's misery that Christianity must direct itself, and it will be the function of the next chapter to consider the universal problems of human life as these have been raised in the universally significant literature of man. We must understand these problems as they affect the total life of humanity unless we are willing to declare our own irrelevance to the human situation. If Christianity has universal validity, it is because it resolves the basic questions of man's relationships to life, in a resolution which is not, to be sure, philosophical and definitive but which is rather, in a somewhat hackneyed word, existential. The basic questions, as they have been perennially raised, concern certain human relationships. First, perhaps, is the relationship of man to death: does man's inevitable and conclusive finiteness imply meaninglessness and futility throughout his life? Then there is his relationship to nature: does man's undenied and inescapable partnership in nature imply as in Lear's words that "man's life is cheap as beast's" and determined in the same way?[58] Finally, there is the relationship of man to himself: does man exist in prison to himself, is his future in bondage to his past, without hope of release to something or someone beyond himself? We will now turn to the literary posing and clarification of these problems.

Chapter Three

LITERATURE AND THE
LIMITS OF MAN

I. *The Issues of Human Misery*

Adapting an insight of Pascal's, and observing that man
cannot be understood apart from his greatness and his misery,
we may say that the preceding chapter was largely concerned
with the manner in which literature discloses and nourishes
human greatness, while in this chapter we will be basically
concerned with the nature of man's misery.

All the races and nations of men having been made of one
blood, of one common nature, we would expect that there is
a universal truth to human life with which all profound
analysis would have to deal. It is this, of course, which we
have found to be the concern of literature, for literature, as
William Faulkner put it, deals with "the old universal truths
lacking which any story is ephemeral and doomed." "The
poet's, the writer's, duty is to write about these things,"
Faulkner continued. "It is his privilege to help man endure
by lifting his heart, by reminding him of the courage and
honor and hope and pride and compassion and pity and
sacrifice which has been the glory of his past. The poet's voice
need not merely be the record of man, it can be one of the

props, the pillars to help him endure and prevail."[1] The writer's contribution to man's greatness could not be better summarized than in those words from Faulkner's acceptance of the Nobel Prize.

And yet we find, above and beyond all of this, that humanity is inclosed in mystery, and when men have, like Tennyson's Ulysses, pressed to the utmost bound of human thought they discover that

> all experience is an arch wherethro'
> Gleams that untravell'd world whose margin fades
> For ever and for ever when I move.[2]

At this point humanity is no longer united by the truth of the answers it gives but rather by the truth of the questions it raises. Until these questions are asked, man lives only in the fool's paradise of Franz Kafka's *The Trial,* where the hero moves through his own mysterious accusation, trial, and condemnation without ever quite asking the basic questions as to his own life, death, and guilt. In one sense, the discovery and posing of the universal human questions are basic to all else in life and thought.

If the action of God through Christ is of universal relevance, as Christians believe, it is because God has acted in response to universal human need. When we say that Christianity is universally applicable to man's condition, we mean, I take it, that in Christ, God has responded in a unique way to issues which are at the base of all human life. If this is not so, then Christianity should not be proclaimed to all men as the means of salvation. And if it is true, then it cannot be understood apart from the universal human issues which are met by the grace of God through the Christian faith.

Literature, by virtue of its function as a mirror held up to man's soul, makes clear what these basic issues are, and it

does so with an immediacy and vitality rarely found in other
approaches to the human situation. If, then, we are to see
clearly the ultimate problems of man's life for which Christian truth must have relevance if it has value, we can scarcely
do better than to study man as his lot is clarified through
enduring literature, where human greatness and misery are
inextricably interrelated. We will explore man's need in
terms of three issues, which do not exhaust the subject but
will clarify it. These are: first the issue posed for life by
death, then the issue for human identity of the relation
between human nature and nature as a whole, and finally the
issue of man's relation to his own failure and guilt.

II. *The Issue of Death*

The issue of death may be posed in this manner: Does the
fact of death as the inescapable finis to life imply a continuous
negation of all of man's existence as meaninglessness and futility? Putting the problem in this way diverts attention from the
relatively short final moments or days of life, in which a man
is said to be "dying," and focuses instead upon the relevance
of death, as finality, for the entire course of life and all that
life involves. Death, in this sense, is a constant feature of life,
and we die daily, even continuously, as all things come to an
end within our lives. No man exists in a constant state of
plenitude and euphoria, but in a persistent movement from
one condition to another: fullness ends in satiety or in hunger, peace in conflict or in ennui, and pleasure in boredom or
in suffering, as death throws a pall over the whole of life.
Though we may be far from Death itself, we walk constantly
through the valley of its shadow.

The implicit concern with death is one that is encountered
wherever the human condition is profoundly considered. We

can hear the Sumerian "Job" crying out some thirty-five hundred years ago in a timeless and intensely human lament, "Food is all about me, yet my food is hunger," and again, "Suffering overwhelms me like one chosen for nothing but tears."[3] Or there is the beautiful and poignant Aztec line, "Our life is like the warming of oneself in the sun."[4] This phrase from the subtropics finds its counterpart in the bleak conception of the Anglo-Saxon thane who described life as being like a stray sparrow flying by chance through a banquet hall in the depth of a northern winter, in at one door and out at another, so that "in the twinkling of an eye the lull for him is over," and he flies from the winter storm back to winter again; "so this life of man appeareth for a little time; but what cometh after, or what went before, we know not."[5] All of life is thus subjected to the curse of transitoriness for, as the Epistle to the Hebrews has it, men through the fear of death are subject to lifelong bondage.[6] It would be difficult to find a more hauntingly beautiful treatment of this perennial theme than in the words of Sophocles' *Oedipus at Colonus:*

> only to gods in heaven
> Comes no old age nor death of anything;
> All else is turmoiled by our master Time.
> The earth's strength fades and manhood's glory fades,
> Faith dies, and unfaith blossoms like a flower.
> And who shall find in the open streets of men
> Or secret places of his own heart's love
> One wind blow true for ever?[7]

In the face of this everlasting transiency, this continuous finitude, the Roman poet Horace hoped that he might make his own life self-sufficient: "I will my own self make my spirit undisturbed,"[8] he wrote. But even so beautiful a hope is ultimately futile, for no man is an island, and all men must anchor their lives in persons and institutions and ideas which soon may be no more. The shadows of loss lies over all of life. Men look behind them and seek the cities of past greatness, to ask with the ancient Egyptian poet, "What are their places now? Their walls are crumbled, their places are nonexistent, as if they had never been," or they meditate like the Old English poet upon the ruins of Roman Britain:

> Desolate now are the courts, and the dome,
> With arches discolored, is stripped of its tiles.
> Where of old once the warrior walked in his pride,
> Gleaming with gold and wanton with wine,
> Splendidly shining in glittering mail,
> The structure lies fallen and shattered in ruin.[9]

Life itself need not be lost—and need not even be near to its end—in order to lose its meaning. So, Creon cries out his misery in Sophocles' *Antigone:*

> Whatever my hands have touched has come to nothing.
> Fate has brought my pride to a thought of dust.[10]

It may be true, as Longfellow wrote in his poetically inferior "Psalm of Life," that

> Life is real! Life is earnest!
> And the grave is not its goal;
> Dust thou art, to dust returnest,
> Was not spoken of the soul.[11]

The Greeks would generally have agreed with Longfellow that immortality and not dust was the goal of human life, although any self-respecting Greek would have deplored Longfellow's jog trot verse. But Creon would surely have found the sententious "Dust thou art, to dust returnest, Was not spoken of the soul" quite irrelevant to his own immediate despair. When Creon says that all his pride has been brought to a thought of dust, he is speaking of *this* life, the here and now, which has been so shattered by the loss of his son, his wife, and his self-respect that life now seems to him to be no more than dust. His whole existence is subjected to bondage and futility by the fact of death. But the most crucial statement of the manner in which the shadow of death casts a blight over life comes from Shakespeare's Macbeth, for whom the whole of life becomes so subject to death that it is virtually meaningless:

> Tomorrow, and tomorrow, and tomorrow,
> Creeps in this petty pace from day to day
> To the last syllable of recorded time;
> And all our yesterdays have lighted fools
> The way to dusty death. Out, out, brief candle!
> Life's but a walking shadow, a poor player,
> That struts and frets his hour upon the stage
> And then is heard no more. It is a tale
> Told by an idiot, full of sound and fury,
> Signifying nothing.[12]

Here the problem of death is so centrally posed that it seems to reduce to dust the activities of every living day.

Beyond this problem of what death implies for man while he lives, there is a second problem, the problem of what death leaves of man when he dies. Again Shakespeare sums the matter up through one of his dramatic characters:

> Ay, but to die, and go we know not where;
> To lie in cold obstruction and to rot;
> This sensible warm motion to become
> A kneaded clod. . . .
> . . . 'Tis too horrible!
> The weariest and most loathed worldly life
> That age, ache, penury, and imprisonment
> Can lay on nature is a paradise
> To what we fear of death.[13]

III. *The Issue of Identity*

In addition to the issue of death, there is the issue of human identity, as man's human nature is considered in the context of nature as a whole. That man is at least in some measure a part of nature never has been, and probably never can be, seriously denied. He is made only a little lower than the angels, and yet he is like the beasts that perish, as the psalmist writes.[14] How then does he establish his own identity, and what is the norm of his action? Time and again throughout history men have assumed that they may find the ultimate source of their identity and the ultimate norm of their actions in conformity to nature. In our own time, particularly, a rather glib assumption runs through much of life and thought to the effect that man may solve the problems which life poses for him simply by "doing what comes naturally" as the Rodgers and Hammerstein song has it. But modern men, even relatively sophisticated modern men who hold that man should seek his well-being in some form of naturalistic conformity, rarely raise the really basic question as to man's relation to nature: To what nature shall man conform? To what has been traditionally understood as distinctively human nature, or to a wild and animal nature? The problem is as perennial as nature itself, and cannot sensibly be overlooked, for an appeal to nature—even to the libido—does not solve man's problems, but implicitly raises the most basic problem of human identity. In the face of this issue, it is shallow indeed to assume that something significant has been said when man is told to satisfy nature, or to "act naturally": the really momentous question is whether we shall pattern ourselves upon nature red in tooth and claw, the nature of blood and iron which Adolph Hitler followed, or upon a nature more closely approximated to what Albert Schweitzer represents.

But though this antithesis is useful, it oversimplifies the problem: Schweitzer's reverence for life is not the only antithesis to the law of the jungle, and we wish to see the problem posed in more inclusive ways.

We find a rudimentary approach made in George Bernard Shaw's *Back to Methuselah,* when Adam and Cain debate as to which of them represents a true and natural manhood, Adam by cultivating the earth in the planting and nurture of life or Cain by imitating the predatory beasts in the destruction of life. But Shaw does not pursue the antithesis in any very extensive way. In Shakespeare's *King Lear,* however, we find a profound and extended exploration of the question as to whether there is any norm of human nature apart from the norm of bloody predation which governs the rest of animal nature. Lear, tortured by the cruelty of his daughters, agonizingly poses the central question: "Is there any cause in nature that makes these hard hearts?"[15]

You will recall that Lear abdicates the throne of Britain in favor of his daughters Goneril and Regan, who later repudiate him, turn him out into the storm, and even seek his life. In contrast to Goneril and Regan is Cordelia, Lear's faithful daughter, who returns to save her father despite the fact that he has peremptorily cast her off. Then, in a subplot which parallels and reinforces the main action, there are the Earl of Gloucester and his two sons, the treacherous and illegitimate Edmund and the faithful, legitimate son Edgar. Gloucester, like Lear, places his trust in the treacherous child and repudiates the faithful child, only to find himself betrayed by the false son he trusted and saved by the child he had himself repudiated. The patterns of acceptance and rejection, established with Lear and repeated with Gloucester, underscore the differences between the decisive views of nature which the children hold and in a manner represent.

Now a great deal more can of course be made of *King Lear*

than we are able to make of it here, but for our present purposes we will be trying to see the manner in which man's
relation to nature is examined. A close reading of the text
will disclose at least two very distinct views of nature as man
is related to it, and these two views are set in opposition to
each other throughout the play. Goneril, Regan, and Edmund the Bastard hold to a view of man's place in nature
according to which man patterns his actions upon the law of
the jungle. In contrast, the sympathetic characters, Cordelia,
Edgar, Kent, and Albany, as well as the gradually enlightened
Lear and Gloucester, view human nature as having a very
distinct and different quality from that of the predatory ani-
mals and the forces of inanimate nature. Thus Shakespeare
dramatically poses the problem as to which nature is proper
to man.

The different views are catalyzed through the two sons of
the Earl of Gloucester. The most extensively defined appeal
to the brutality of nature as a pattern for man's endeavor
comes from Edmund, whom Shakespeare has carefully made
an illegitimate son—or, as the Elizabethans said, a "natural"
son—so that he would not only hold to but in good measure
represent a particular view of the natural as animal-like
satisfaction of instinctual drives. In a significant soliloquy
Edmund develops his conception of nature as predatory and
libidinous and then takes this nature of the jungle as his
goddess:

> Thou, Nature, art my goddess; to thy law
> My services are bound.[16]

His actions, thereafter, are to disgrace his brother by treachery
and drive him into exile so as to succeed to his inheritance.
He then proceeds to the betrayal of his father so that he succeeds to the title itself while Gloucester is turned out to
wander in blind helplessness with a sentence of death upon
his head. Finally, Edmund plots to accomplish his own ac-

cession to the rule of England by paying adulterous court to both Goneril and Regan. So, relying upon what he calls "the lusty stealth of nature . . . and fierce quality," he advances himself, until at the end of the play "the wheel is come full circle" and he is killed in tourney by his legitimate brother Edgar.[17]

At the opposite pole from Edmund is Edgar, the legitimate brother who is reduced to the utmost in human misery and who preserves his life and that of his father by assuming the disguise of a madman, "poor Tom o' Bedlam." As the insane Tom, he accepts Lear into his miserable hovel during the storm, and in his purposed and reasoned irrationality he states the case against any patterning of human nature upon the nature of the jungle. Edgar treats what his brother ascribes to the goddess Nature as being in reality the province of the demonic, of "the foul fiend" who leads man through a course of pain which closely approximates the experiences to which Lear and Gloucester are subjected by their unkind children:

> through fire and through flame, through ford and whirlpool, o'er bog and quagmire; that hath laid knives under his pillow and halters in his pew, set ratsbane by his porridge, made him proud of heart, to ride on a bay trotting horse over four-inch'd bridges, to course his own shadow for a traitor.[18]

The effect of the fiend is precisely what we find in Edmund, Goneril, and Regan, the followers of natural law of the animal kingdom, who introduce into the kingdom of man unbridled lust, pride, treachery to parents and to each other, and who attempt to live on the human plane like the "hog in sloth, fox in stealth, wolf in greediness, dog in madness, lion in prey." All of which is, according to the sanely counterfeited madness of Edgar, the province of the prince of darkness who "hurts the poor creature of earth."[19]

The Lear to whom Edgar says these things is a tremendously confused and distraught old man. Caught up between the fierceness of a storm which he instinctively feels to be natural and proper, and the equal ferocity of daughters whom he instinctively regards as "unnatural," Lear finds his spirit stretched out upon a rack of uncertainty, torment, and misery. As he feels himself drawn toward madness, Lear finds a kindred spirit in the miserable and apparently mad beggar whose hovel he shares, and to whom he listens with the closest attention as Edgar in the words of "foolishness" sets forth a wisdom which seems to the old king far more profound than that of the worldly-wise court circle of Goneril, Regan, and Edmund. The effect upon Lear is that he now finds a resolution to the tension between two views of nature, as in Edgar he discovers a human nature which is far different from the nature of wild and unfeeling forces. "Thou art the thing itself," he says to Edgar; "unaccommodated man is no more but such a poor, bare, forked animal as thou art."[20] Man is still an animal, but an animal with a difference, and he must follow what is good and proper within the particular sphere of a distinctively human nature, rather than what is good and proper only within the sphere of the lower orders of nature. To pattern his life on a nature lower than his own is to yield to the prince of darkness.

Earlier Lear had cried out, under the humiliation to which Goneril subjected him, "Who is it that can tell me who I am?"[21] Now, after great suffering, the recognition of what human nature is—"the thing itself"—leads him through further suffering to further recognition. By suffering he comes to know the falsity of that regal flattery which he had once enjoyed because it told him that he was above nature: "I am not ague-proof," he says, and "the thunder would not peace at my bidding."[22] He accepts his place in nature, but even more importantly he accepts his common humanity, his bond with all men, as he wipes his hand before extending it for the blind Gloucester to kiss, for "it smells of mortality."[23] It is in this scene, where he is clad only in weeds and reduced to "unaccommodated man," that he declares himself "every inch a king."[24] And he still has one daughter, the faithful Cordelia, "who redeems nature from the general curse"[25] and who by her humane filial love reclaims Lear himself from madness and despair. Similarly in the subplot it was Edgar, the embodiment of normatively human nature, in opposition to Edmund, the follower of the goddess Nature, who cared for the blind Gloucester, "led him, begg'd for him, sav'd him from despair," so that at the end his heart "burst smilingly."[26]

The play *King Lear* does not end on any rousing affirmation of joy, however, but rather on a muted note of sadness. Perhaps a final affirmation is not needed, for the play itself has so clearly treated its problem that it carries within itself the assurance that man's life is not as cheap as beast's, however much men may try to make it so by repudiating humane nature and adhering to the law of predation. On the other hand, there is a sense in which no real affirmation is possible in this play, for although Lear dies as a noble and tragic figure, the struggle which is depicted in his life is an unending one and will be repeatedly engaged in throughout human history. His own experience has not affected that basic struggle in the least; it has only clarified what is involved in it. Kent speaks against the attempt to coax Lear into any longer life:

> O, let him pass! He hates him
> That would upon the rack of this tough world
> Stretch him out longer.[27]

But it is Albany, the successor to Lear's crown, who speaks the decisive word: "Our present business Is general woe."[28] Lear's struggle is over, but the struggle of all men to find and to assert the norm of their own existence, of their human nature, continues unaffected and uneased. The tension for man between the conception of a distinctive human nature and the encroaching, ever-threatening, ever-predatory norm of a nature red in tooth and claw is a tension from which he cannot entirely free himself and which he cannot finally dissolve by and for himself. He can suffer these tensions with nobility, but he can escape them only through death, unless there is some rescue, some incursion of hope from outside; and of that there is no sign at the close of *King Lear*. I know of no words which more aptly indicate our state of mind at the end of this tragedy than the words of Pascal, when he describes a "doubtful ambiguity and in a certain doubtful dimness from which our doubts cannot take away all the clearness, nor our own natural lights chase away all the darkness. . . . The greatness of man is great in that he knows himself to be miserable. A tree does not know itself to be miserable. It is then being miserable to know oneself to be miserable; but it is also being great to know that one is miserable. All these same miseries prove man's greatness. They are the miseries of a great lord, of a deposed king."[29] Pascal pointed out that the only possible reconciliation of man's greatness and his misery, without pride and without despair, is through Jesus Christ. But Lear's world was a pagan world, and we are not yet ready to go on to the literary treatment of man in a purely and distinctively Christian perspective.

IV. *The Issue of Failure and Guilt*

Much modern literature has to do with the misery and greatness of the average or below-average man. The classic pattern is different, for it focuses upon misery and greatness in the most outstanding and heroic men. The classical test cases are thus more catalytic of human misery, and treat its presence in those who carry the human enterprise to the farthest limits of character and achievement. Even at the zenith of human accomplishment, man is cursed by an ultimate failure to establish his greatness at a point beyond the reaches of human misery. In the literary masterpieces to which men return century after century because they find in them truth to the universally human condition, there are few ultimately successful heroes. The Tarzans, the Supermen, the bright and always undefeated heroes, are figments suited to television and Hollywood, fit only for diverting man from his ultimate problems and not for helping him to face them. But in the great tradition of literature even the most titanic heroes rarely escape the misery of man's lot by the power of man's own greatness.

The most ancient of all known epics appears to be the Mesopotamian *Epic of Gilgamesh,* which is thought to have been composed early in the second millennium B.C.[30] In it, Gilgamesh and his adopted brother Enkidu are unmatched among men and gods. All goes down before their seemingly irresistible might. And then Enkidu dies, and Gilgamesh, who has known death and defeat only as abstract possibilities, must now face their stark, concrete reality when he finds that "he who with me has shared all hazards, the fate of man has overtaken." He vainly calls upon Enkidu to arise:

My friend, my younger brother—who with me in the foothills
Hunted wild ass, and panther in the plains;
Enkidu, my friend, my younger brother—who with me in the
    foothills
Hunted wild ass, and panther in the plains;
Who with me could do all, who climbed the crags,
Seized, killed the bull of heaven,
Flung down Huwawa, dwelling in the cedar forest.
Now—what sleep is this that seized you?
You have grown dark and cannot hear me.[31]

The horror of death now preoccupies Gilgamesh's mind, so that he sets out to find and to seize for himself the plant of immortality. He is warned by all who meet him that his task is futile:

> Gilgamesh, whither are you wandering?
> Life, which you look for, you will never find.
> For when the gods created man, they let
> Death be his share, and life
> Withheld in their own hands.[32]

Gilgamesh nonetheless persists until he does find the plant of everlasting rejuvenation, and with it journeys back toward his home. But, exhausted from his heroic struggles, he cannot resist the temptation offered by a cool lake. Plunging in to refresh himself from the unremitting efforts which had won the plant of life, he loses the plant itself, and all that is left him are the tears of bitterness.

When we come to the *Iliad* we find a considerably more sophisticated epic than *Gilgamesh,* but here again we encounter the persistent patterns of human misery. The greatest man in either of the contending forces, Greek or Trojan, is clearly the Trojan Hector, supreme both as a warrior who was the mainspring of all Trojan effort—"only Hector guarded Ilios"—and as a noble human being, beside whom Odysseus seemed only a clever schemer and Achilles a fighting animal. And yet when Hector goes outside the walls of Troy for the final encounter, this man whose courage and skill were proverbial finds all his mighty resources dissolving into nothingness. He is no longer the emblem of triumphant human greatness but rather becomes the image of all human greatness shocked and numbed by the awful recognition of its own limitation. He flies hopelessly from the pursuing Achilles, not because it helps him to do so, but only because all the power that is left him is the power of flight, and even this is futile.

And then there is *Beowulf,* the Anglo-Saxon epic which is in some ways, I believe, almost as great a work as the *Iliad.* Beowulf, like Hector and Gilgamesh, is the undefeated ideal of his society, but when he plunges into the dark tarn of monsters to destroy the murderous, demonic sea-troll who has harried and killed the Danish people, Beowulf quickly comes to the limit of his powers. His own humanly designed sword will not cut through to the life of his adversary. Final victory comes, not through the strength of Beowulf's arm, but through a divine sword revealed, as the Christian poet says, by the grace of God, by the use of which alone Beowulf can slay the monster.[33] The point, clearly enough, is that man's ultimate extremity is relieved through God, rather than through his own powers. Beowulf could with his own hand destroy the lesser monster Grendel, but when he came to encounter the greater parent and origin of Grendel's power in the sea-troll, he was helpless apart from grace. Beowulf's victory, as he himself declares, is not a victory in the common moral or physical sense, but is rather a gift. Beowulf succeeded, where Lear failed, in his battle with nature and with the demonic not because his heart was purer than the heart of Lear, but because he, like Gideon, fought with the sword of the Lord.

The examples which we have cited thus far—Gilgamesh, Hector, and Beowulf—all involve men of action who are only incidentally men of thought and who therefore do not subject their own lives to prolonged and profoundly thoughtful scrutiny. What we now need to find is a man who in nobility and wisdom stands at the pinnacle of human achievement and who, in that situation, examines the scope and meaning of his life with intelligence and absolute honesty. We find such a man in Sophocles' *Oedipus the King*, and here what we have already noted as a sense of failure in the man of action deepens into a sense of guilt in the man of thought.

Oedipus is the solver of riddles par excellence, who is destroyed by the riddle of his own life. He has repeatedly been taken as a universal human symbol, as a type of every-man, and it is in this sense that he is presented in Sophocles' play. As the Chorus puts it,

All the generations of mortal man add up to nothing!
Show me the man whose happiness was anything more than
  illusion
Followed by disillusion.
Here is the instance, here is Oedipus, here is the reason
Why I call no mortal creature happy.[34]

Underscoring this point, one of the leading scholars of Greek tragedy, H. D. F. Kitto, writes of Oedipus that he is not a special case but is "as the Chorus says, typical; what has happened to him is part of the whole web of human life."[35]

Oedipus was the son of Laius, king of Thebes, and his queen Jocasta. When an oracle warned that the son would kill his father, the infant Oedipus was ordered to be exposed to the elements, and so killed. The servant to whom this task was entrusted, however, secretly gave the child to an-other retainer, who in turn presented Oedipus to the king and queen of Corinth, by whom he was reared as a son. Without knowledge of his origin, Oedipus grew to manhood and heard from the oracle of Delphi that if he did not stay away from his home he would kill his father and marry his mother. Terrified, he turned his back upon the court of Corinth and made his way to Thebes, thus, unknowingly, going to the home which was to be his doom and thus be-coming involved in the very evil which he sought to evade. On the way to Thebes he met a stranger accompanied by a number of retainers. A quarrel developed in which Oedipus killed them all, unaware that the stranger was his father, King Laius. Upon his arrival in Thebes, Oedipus found the city cursed by the presence of a monster, the Sphinx, who devoured all who could not answer her riddle. Oedipus, however, defied the dangers involved and gave the proper answer to the Sphinx, who then destroyed herself.

Oedipus has thus freed Thebes from the predations of the monster, and, as the throne has recently been made vacant by the unexpected and mysterious death of King Laius, Oedipus is made king. Following the established and ancient customs of kingship, he is married to the widowed queen. No one involved knows of their relationship to each other. A number of years later pestilence and famine threaten to destroy the city because, as the oracle reveals, Laius' murderer lives within Thebes undetected and unpunished. The people appeal to Oedipus to deliver them, and he agrees to do so by discovering for himself the murderer who has polluted his city. The unraveling of this mystery constitutes the action of Sophocles' drama *Oedipus the King*. With the unremitting thoroughness of a modern detective, Oedipus pursues every clue, follows every possible line of inquiry, and as he does so he finds, gradually accumulating, incontrovertible evidence that he is himself the polluter of his city, the sinister and damning influence which he seeks.

That, in brief, is the story of Oedipus as it concerns us here. In mid-twentieth century, however, we are generally less familiar with the story itself than we are with Sigmund Freud's interpretation of it. In Freud's words, "Oedipus, who slew his father Laius and wedded his mother Jocasta, is nothing more or less than a wish-fulfillment—the fulfillment of the wish of our childhood."[36] In terms of this analysis, then, Oedipus represents primarily the sexual attraction which the male child feels for his mother along with a concomitant antagonism to his father—a condition which Freud regards as virtually universal—and it is here that Freud would have us find the universal significance of King Oedipus.

It would be false to assume that Freud represents the only word of psychology on this subject. As is well known, Alfred Adler dismissed the Oedipus complex outright as a part of what he derisively called the Freudian "mythology of sex," while Erich Fromm in his *The Forgotten Language* has marshaled certain very telling and, from the point of view of purely literary analysis, indeed irrefutable evidence against Freud's interpretation of Sophocles' text. Fromm states his case in this way:

> There is no indication whatsoever in the myth that Oedipus is attracted by or falls in love with Jocasta. The only reason we are given for Oedipus's marriage to Jocasta is that she, as it were, goes with the throne. Should we believe that a myth, the central theme of which [allegedly] constitutes an incestuous relationship between mother and son, would entirely omit the element of attraction between the two?[37]

Fromm then proceeds to cite Oedipus' own declaration in *Oedipus at Colonus* to the effect that he had not sought Jocasta to be his bride, but that she was given to him by the city as part and parcel of his accession to the throne,[38] a very significant piece of evidence which Freud appears to have overlooked entirely. All in all, at least for the psychological analyses of Oedipus with which I am familiar, the most responsible from a literary point of view are those of the Adlerian type which interpret the issues of the drama primarily in terms of power, as Fromm does, rather than of incest. But this is not to deny the existence of the complex which Freud attached, wrongly I think, to Oedipus' name: the phenomenon may exist, even though it has been misnamed.

But the basic understanding of *Oedipus the King* is far more profound than either Fromm or Freud suggests, and for this understanding we would do well to turn from the famous psychologists to the sounder but less well known literary critics. Professor Kitto thus speaks of the importance of Sophocles' emphasis on *phronesis*, or "wisdom," which "implies knowing what you are, knowing your place in the world, being able to take the wide view, with a due sense of proportion."[39] The meaning or spiritual content of *Oedipus the King* in this more inclusive sense, as Francis Fergusson has aptly phrased it, "is the tragic action which Sophocles directly presents; and this action is in its essence *zweideutig*: triumph and destruction, darkness and enlightenment, mourning and rejoicing, at any moment we care to consider it."[40] The tragic ambiguities of even the noblest human life thus again appear upon the center of the stage as we see man in his greatness and his misery.

The focus of *Oedipus the King* is upon the ultimate mystery of the human situation, but the drama itself never arrives at a solution to that ultimate mystery. As for the proximate mystery—who is the polluter of the city?—that is solved, but it is solved in a way which serves to underscore the universal riddles of human *Zweideutigkeit*: greatness and misery.

There is no question as to Oedipus' stature. The Chorus calls him "greatest of men," and it is to him that the citizens look as their first hope of deliverance from pollution.[41] To him the priest appeals, calling him

> the first of men
> Whether in the ordinary business of mortal life,
> Or in the encounters of man with more than man.[42]

Reminding him of the wisdom with which he had broken "our bondage to the vile Enchantress," the priest continues with a new appeal that Oedipus save his people:

> Now, Oedipus great and glorious, we seek
> Your help again. Find some deliverance for us
> By any way that god or man can show.[43]

Oedipus' response is that of the just and responsible ruler: "I will start afresh and bring everything into the light," he promises. He places a sentence on the head of the unknown guilty one, and then he adds: "Nor do I exempt myself from the imprecation."[44]

The task of Oedipus, then, is the task of every man: to find the guilt which mars and preys upon himself and upon his human community. The importance of this fact can scarcely be overstated, for Sophocles has in Oedipus dramatized the greatest and wisest of men seeking the cause of human ruin. And he finds that cause, not in another as he expects, but to his horror and despairing dismay he finds it in himself. At first he resists the process of unmasking and refuses to recognize his own guilt, as the blind prophet Tiresias taunts him with the fact that he has eyes but will not see his own guilt. His inherent honesty, however, prevents him from escaping the conclusion which his justice has led him to seek, and he accepts the proof of Tiresias' charge that "you are yourself the murderer that you seek," and "you are your own enemy."[45]

Oedipus, who had valiantly declared "I ask to be no other man Than that I am, and will know who I am," now discovers in himself "all human filthiness in one crime compounded."[46] "On me," he cries, "is the curse that none but I have laid,"[47] as his honesty and justice force him into self-recognition and self-judgment. Oedipus represents the highest achievements of a purely human nature, the far projection of the ideal of a distinctively humane order of life. But that is not enough, and Oedipus finds himself betrayed by himself, blinded by himself, bound by himself. Here is that eternal note of human sadness, of which Matthew Arnold wrote:

> Sophocles long ago
> Heard it on the Aegean and it brought
> Into his mind the turbid ebb and flow
> Of human misery.[48]

Man recognizes the impasse of human effort, from which there seems to be no way by which he can work his own escape. But this recognition comes only under certain conditions: Oedipus could have evaded it had his sense of justice allowed him to ignore, as Jocasta urges him to do, the accumulating evidences of his own guilt. He could have avoided it entirely had he not been impelled by his intransigent honesty to seek and to know the truth. Tiresias the seer, who knows of Oedipus' unsuspected crimes, at first refuses to answer Oedipus' questions as to who pollutes the city, and persists in this refusal until Oedipus, like a skilled and ruthless prosecutor, goads, taunts, and even insults him into telling all that he knows. Others also seek to protect Oedipus from the consequences of his own inquiry; but, impelled both by justice and honesty, Oedipus persists for, as he says, "I cannot leave the truth unknown."[49] His greatness compels him to recognize his misery and then to declare "I have committed such heinous sin As no mere death could pay for."[50]

It is at some such point as this, when human greatness has unflinchingly recognized human misery, that the Christian faith becomes ultimately relevant to man. Apart from that recognition, however, the Christian message is quite unintelligible and may even seem quite pointless. If a man shuts himself off from human nature and can make himself content with the goddess of wild and animal nature, he will be unaware of any need for the grace of God. But even beyond that, if he lives his life on a high plane of distinctively human value without looking too closely at himself, without unmasking himself, he may still remain unconscious of any basic impasse in his existence. It is only when, Oedipus-like, he has in honesty and justice recognized himself as the polluter whom he seeks, that he is prepared to understand his own passion and the relevance to it of the passion of Christ.

This recognition by Oedipus of the human impasse is not

PART III

The Literature
of Redemption

Chapter Four

THE PATTERNS OF
CHRISTIAN REDEMPTION

I. *The Emerging Hope*

In the last chapter we discussed three crucial issues with which man is confronted by his experience of life. Death continuously threatens him, and the threat is no less when it directly concerns not his own life but the life of persons or things or institutions which he loves. And by death, as well as by birth, he is joined into a common lot with all of nature, so that he must somehow determine where the norm and standard of his own distinctively human nature lies. Finally, even when he assumes and achieves for himself a high mark of human greatness, he fails in his strength, and if he is given to the human honesty and justice of Oedipus, he admits that "on me is the curse that none but I have laid."[1] Man may not avoid that awful recognition by some feasible and facile effort to be greater or more prudent than Oedipus, for Oedipus represents a maximal type of human greatness and wisdom, as the Chorus reiterates; man may avoid it only by a repudiation of honesty—an abandonment of Oedipus' determination to know the truth—or by a repudiation of justice—

an abandonment of Oedipus' profound human integrity in judging the truth he knows. If man abandons his distinctively human qualities, he finds himself no longer a man, and yet if he adheres to them he finds himself unable to live by them. Oedipus' attendant laments that

> Not all the waters of Ister, the waters of Phasis,
> Can wash this dwelling clean of the foulness within.[2]

And the apostle Paul speaks of the universal human anguish when he too cries out, "O wretched man that I am! who shall deliver me from the body of this death?"[3] Escape is impossible; the only hope is for deliverance, or there is no hope. For Oedipus there was none:

> O dark intolerable inescapable night
> That has no day!
> Cloud that no air can take away![4]

And the Old English poet echoes the same darkness, though now with a new hope, as he prays to God for the wretched men

> Who in this dark dungeon sit here sad
> Through all the sweet journey of the sun

and

> who have long been sitting
> Attired with darkness in eternal night,
> Where clothed with sin and covered with shadows
> They needs must endure Death's dark shade.[5]

The brilliant darkness of the Greek poet is matched by that of the Anglo-Saxon, but for the latter there is hope, and beyond hope, assurance, for his poem is written of Christ:

> As thou wast once begotten God of God,
> True Son of the Father, before all ages
> For ever Lord in celestial light,
> So now in need Thy work doth beseech Thee
> Send the bright sun and come Thyself.

In the incarnation God responds to man's impasse:

> He brings thee bliss,
> Looses thy bondage, draws nigh unto men,
> For He only knows their harrowing need,
> How man in his wretchedness waits upon mercy.[6]

The limited extent of man's endeavor in his human impasse is to pray for mercy and for grace. In Christopher Fry's recent play, *A Sleep of Prisoners,* three captured soldiers dream that they are a modern trio of Shadrac, Meshac, and Abednego, caught up in a very contemporary fiery furnace. In the semiclarity of a dream world, they find that their hands are tied behind their backs so that they cannot stand at attention, while their feet are hobbled so that they cannot stand at ease. There is no hope of escape, and in a situation where neither attention nor ease is possible, their corporal, Adams, says:

> That leaves me without a word of command
> To cover the situation, except
> Fall on your knees.[7]

They do so, and in the heat of "a fire hotter Than any fire has ever been" they find that they still live. Corporal Adams speaks again, this time in words which unconsciously seem to form a Christian-existential antithesis to Descartes' "I think, therefore I am." Adams wonderingly declares: "I live. I know I kneel."[8]

Then in the flames of this modern furnace, as in Daniel's furnace, there appears a mysterious fourth figure. Fry has his advent heralded by an old symbol, the crowing cock, the symbol of the presence of Christ. Corporal Adams—"the old Adam" in this play—asks "Who are you?" and the stranger replies, simply, "Man." "Under what command?" Adams persists, and the reply comes back, "God's." As they converse, enlightenment dawns upon Adams and as he now recognizes the full significance of the incarnation he explodes with the utterly astonished question,

> You cockeyed son
> Of heaven, how did you get here?

"Under the fence," the son of heaven replies, for he chose to come on his own initiative. In response to the question "Who's to lead us out of this?" the Christ-figure replies by asking another question, the question of man's relation to his own past, "Who will trust What the years have endlessly said?"

> Behind us lie
> The thousand and the thousand and the thousand years
> Vexed and terrible. And still we use
> The cures which never cure.

The solution does not lie there, in the endlessly repeated exploits and rituals of human ingenuity, nor does it lie in the naturalistic self-assertion of the individual who seeks his own salvation apart from the good of the entire body of men:

> But there's not a skipping soul
> On the loneliest goat-path who is not
> Hugged into this, the human shambles.
> And whatever happens on the farthest pitch,
> To the sand-man in the desert or the island-man in the sea,
> Concerns us very soon.

And the problem of mortality—"Each man who dies, Dies the world with him"—is not only a problem in itself for us, but as we respond to it we respond in terms of increasing sin so that we need to pray even here, "O forgive us our deaths in all their ways, Whether of action or of heart." Victory may come, the divine stranger says, when we believe "with a long courage of truth," but one of the prisoners caustically derides the hope of that faith:

> Corporal, the crowing son of heaven
> Thinks we can make a morning.

In reply, the stranger affirms the hope of morning, but denies that man can make it come

> By old measures. Expedience and self-preservation
> Can rot as they will.

But now, the son of heaven says, "the human heart can go the lengths of God," because something radically new has happened:

> Dark and cold we may be, but this
> Is no winter now. The frozen misery
> Of centuries breaks, cracks, begins to move,
> The thunder is the thunder of the floes,
> The thaw, the flood, the upstart Spring.

And that being true, all the other issues are caught up in a great new affirmation of human life and history, which now, despite death and pain and violence and failure and guilt, become filled with meaning and excitement:

> Thank God our time is now when wrong
> Comes up to face us everywhere,
> Never to leave us till we take
> The longest stride of soul men ever took.
> Affairs are now soul size.
> The enterprise
> Is exploration into God,
> Where no nation's foot has ever trodden yet.[9]

II. *The Empty Evasion*

The Christian interpretation of life may be accepted or rejected, and in our time as in every time there is both acceptance and rejection. But I suspect that there have been few times in human history when a larger part of the acceptance was spurious, based upon false considerations. To say that is only to reiterate the concern which many thoughtful Christians feel over popular interpretations of the Christian life as a broad and easy way, perfumed with a cheap aura of the peace of shallow minds. But something else also needs to be said, for if much of the acceptance of Christianity is superficial and wrongly grounded, so too is much of the rejection. We live in an essentially superficial age, where even the intellectuals all too often offer merely a fashionable caricature of thought. To paraphrase Peter de Vries, we may seem profound on the surface, but down deep we are shallow.

Nowhere is this shallowness more graphically described than in the writings of T. S. Eliot. You may recall his poem *The Hollow Men,* the opening of which stands as a summary of modern secularized and one-dimensional culture:

> We are the hollow men
> We are the stuffed men
> Leaning together
> Headpiece filled with straw. Alas!
> Our dried voices, when
> We whisper together
> Are quiet and meaningless
> As wind in dry grass
> Or rats' feet over broken glass
> In our dry cellar.
>
> Shape without form, shade without colour,
> Paralysed force, gesture without motion;
>
> Those who have crossed
> With direct eyes, to death's other Kingdom
> Remember us—if at all—not as lost
> Violent souls, but only
> As the hollow men
> The stuffed men.[10]

The emptiness persists in its own sterility, and seeks to fill its void with the endless, pointless repetition of enterprises which pass for action or for the creation of thought but which are merely the fruitless attempt to fill a vacuum. As Eliot puts it in *Choruses from "The Rock"*: "They write innumerable books; being too vain and distracted for silence: seeking every one after his own elevation, and dodging his emptiness," and "dreaming of systems so perfect that no one will need to be good."[11]

Modern man seeks to protect himself from the recognition of his own impasse and from the dreaded possibility of encounter with God by the perennial repetition in new forms of old devices which have always failed:

> O weariness of men who turn from GOD
> To the grandeur of your mind and the glory of your action,
> To arts and inventions and daring enterprises,
> To schemes of human greatness thoroughly discredited,
> Binding the earth and the water to your service,
> Exploiting the seas and developing the mountains,
> Dividing the stars into common and preferred,
> Engaged in devising the perfect refrigerator,
> Engaged in working out a rational morality,
> Engaged in printing as many books as possible,
> Plotting of happiness and flinging empty bottles,
> Turning from your vacancy to fevered enthusiasm
> For nation or race or what you call humanity.[12]

Eliot's epitaph for our culture is simple and direct. When all lies in ruin, the wind will say:

> Here were decent godless people:
> Their only monument the asphalt road
> And a thousand lost golf balls.[13]

The image of man "dodging his emptiness" is one of Eliot's favorite pictures of modern secularized culture, and he carries this image into a final judgment of man. Man's insistence upon emptiness chains him to it, and when he persistently clings to his isolation until he becomes incapable of anything else, then he is in hell, as Dr. Harcourt-Reilly tells Celia in *The Cocktail Party*.[14] In the same play, Edward, who has himself not yet turned away from the road to hell, describes hell in this way:

> What is hell? Hell is oneself,
> Hell is alone, the other figures in it
> Merely projections. There is nothing to escape from
> And nothing to escape to. One is always alone.[15]

In these lines there is bound up much of the Christian conception of damnation. To apply to the words of the Anglo-Catholic Eliot the conception of the leading Reformed theologian, the death of the soul, as defined by Calvin, is to be without God, "to be abandoned to oneself."[16] The same conception of emptiness and isolation comes out again in the speech of Thomas Becket in Eliot's *Murder in the Cathedral*:

> And behind the Judgement the Void, more horrid than active
>   shapes of hell;
> Emptiness, absence, separation from God;
> The horror of the effortless journey, to the empty land
> Which is no land, only emptiness, absence, the Void,
> Where those who were men can no longer turn the mind
> To distraction, delusion, escape into dream, pretense,
> Where the soul is no longer deceived, for there are no objects,
>   no tones,
> No colours, no forms to distract, to divert the soul
> From seeing itself, foully united forever, nothing with
>   nothing. . . .[17]

In the meanwhile, man frenziedly stuffs and gluts his emptiness with activity, so as to continue the deception, the delusion, that he is competent to fill his own void and fulfill his own being. At all costs he would evade the recognition of his own impasse, and although escape is impossible for him, evasion is possible so long as he lacks either honesty or justice.

III. *The Pattern of Atonement*

When man attains to a considerable measure of honesty and of justice, however, he finds himself in a different situation. No longer able to evade his guilt, he must dissolve it, and for this purpose one or both of two strategies generally come into play: these are the strategy of self-punishment and the strategy of self-ransom. Man attempts to purge his guilt either by punishing himself out of it or by paying himself out of it.

Oedipus follows the strategy of self-punishment when he puts out his own eyes, saying that this was "the best That could have been done," to destroy sight so that his eyes

> should see no longer his shame, his guilt
> No longer see those they should never have seen,
> Nor see, unseeing, those he had longed to see,
> Henceforth seeing nothing but night.[18]

So, too, Shakespeare's Othello passes judgment on himself, regarding suicide as the only course open to him in view of his acknowledged guilt in murdering the innocent Desdemona. And the large part of modern man's masochism and darkly enjoyed self-torture is, I suspect, but a form of the perennial attempt to punish himself because of his own deep-seated and largely subconscious feelings of guilt. This is what we find in Christopher Fry's *The Lady's Not for Burning*, where the disillusioned young war veteran Thomas Mendip seeks his own hanging, accusing himself of being "guilty of mankind," and declaring that "I have perpetrated human

nature." Man's recognition that his life is evil seems inevitably to lead him into attempts at self-punishment. So
Hamlet's thoughts of suicide come both out of his frustration
and out of his recognition that his flesh is "sullied." To return
to *The Lady's Not for Burning,* we find Thomas Mendip
summarizing this archetypal human response in terms of a
formula which we see repeatedly illustrated in human experience: "I defend myself against pain and death by pain
And death."[19]

In George Bernard Shaw's *Major Barbara* there is a char-
acter named Bill Walker, a Cockney workman, whose mistress
leaves him to join the Salvation Army. Infuriated, Bill comes
to get her back, and when he cannot find her, he gives a
severe beating to the first Salvation Army girl he can find.
Afterward he is overcome with an agonizing sense of guilt.
To purge himself, he attempts to give money to the Salvation
Army, so as to buy a way out of his guilty conscience. But
Major Barbara, the heroine of the play, refuses his money.
Then he decides that, in order to purify himself from the
hurt he inflicted on Jenny Hill, he must get himself hurt, so
that by bearing pain his soul will be satisfied. He therefore
determines to spit in the eye of Todger Fairmile, now a Salvation Army sergeant but recently a boxing and wrestling
champion, with the assurance that Fairmile will then beat
the guilt out of him:

> Aw'm gowin to Kennintahn, to spit in Todger Fairmawl's eye.
> Aw beshed Jenny Ill's fice; an nar Aw'll get me aown fice
> beshed and cam beck and shaow it to er. Ee'll itt me ardern
> Aw itt er. That'll mike us square.

He then turns to Adolphus Cusins, a university professor of
Greek and an authority on comparative religion, and asks if
his proposal is just:

> Is that fair or is it not? Youre a genlmn: you oughter knaow.

Cusins at once sees the universality of Walker's solution and declares that "it's exactly what an ancient Greek would have done." To Major Barbara's incredulous question, "But what good will it do?" Cusins replies that "it will give Mr. Fairmile some exercise: and it will satisfy Mr. Walker's soul." Bill Walker's hope is that either by giving payment or by accepting punishment he may arrange things so that, as he put it, all involved would "Let wot Aw dan be dan an pide for; and let there be an end of it."[20]

Now it must be said that the source of Bill's guilt, the original evil from which it sprang, is relatively a peccadillo and surely cannot be taken as catalytic of any very basic insight into human sin, but his response to that evil in terms of guilt and the atonement for guilt does fit into the perennial human pattern as we have seen it developing here. For one reason or another, and in various forms, man recognizes his guilt if he is honest and is concerned to remove it if he is just. To relieve himself—or, as George Bernard Shaw's Professor Cusins says, to satisfy his soul—he seeks to purge himself either by some form of payment or service to others, or by bringing punishment upon himself. Perhaps he does both, or, even more basically, perhaps the two gestures really amount to the same thing—a sacrifice for expiation.

Man's attempt to sacrifice for himself does not bring him the ultimate freedom he seeks, however, because it represents an increasing reliance upon the self and it is precisely from self-reliance that man must be freed. In these terms suicide is the final form of self-assertion, the ultimate self-reliance, the irrevocable assumption that man can judge himself and determine the bounds of his own being. And the seeking of sainthood through martyrdom is little better, as T. S. Eliot's Saint Thomas Becket realizes. Indeed, the attempt to work one's way into favor—whether it be God's favor or one's own—represents a form of the problem itself, rather than its solution. A priest describes Thomas Becket early in *Murder in the Cathedral* in terms of this feeding of sin with virtue:

> His pride always feeding upon his own virtues,
> Pride drawing sustenance from impartiality,
> Pride drawing sustenance from generosity. . . .[21]

Thomas himself is well aware of his dilemma, of the fact that "sin grows with doing good" for "the greatest treason" is "to do the right deed for the wrong reason."[22] His sin is pride, self-love, and self-assertion, but if he attempts to purge himself of this sin by mortification or martyrdom, he has merely indulged a more subtle form of pride. He cries out his agony:

> Is there no way, in my soul's sickness,
> Does not lead to damnation in pride?
> I well know that these temptations
> Mean present vanity and future torment.
> Can sinful pride be driven out
> Only by more sinful? Can I neither act nor suffer
> Without perdition?[23]

He can neither *pay* his way out by acting, nor *punish* his way out by suffering. He is caught in the impasse of man, where no self-atoning sacrifice is possible without compounding the offense.

It is for this reason that man must renounce entirely all that he himself can do to expiate his own guilt. John Milton, in *Paradise Lost*, writes that man must renounce all his own works, whether good or evil, as God the Father declares to God the Son:

> thy merit
> Imputed shall absolve them who renounce
> Their own both righteous and unrighteous deeds,
> And live in thee transplanted, and from thee
> Receive new life.[24]

In *Piers Plowman,* William Langland makes it the central fact of every Christian life that Christ has opened the way of access to God for pilgrims by riding as a knightly champion for man, clearing the highways to God for all time by his passage on the Palestinian roads and by his tournament fought on Calvary.[25] The frustrating futility of all the atonements which man imposes on himself, ceaselessly tormenting himself, are superseded by the one sacrifice of Jesus Christ. No man need ever again be enslaved by the futile attempt to purge himself by pain or by payment, for man's atonement has been made in the very manner in which man seeks to make it but cannot, and man is thus set free when he accepts in faith the fact of this freedom as it is applied to him by God.

The significance of the Celtic cross comes at once to mind. In pre-Christian times, according to an ancient legend, heathen Celtic priests had fixed a circle above an altar of sacrifice, and when the sun shone through that circle so as to strike the center of the altar, the time had come for a new human death, a new attempt at purgation and atonement. When the Christian missionaries arrived, they laid the cross over the circle, to signify the fact that the one sacrifice had been made which obviated the dreadful necessity of all others, whether made by man of men or by a man of himself. Christopher Fry has perfectly caught the spirit of that meaning in his play *Thor, With Angels,* as the Teutonic pagan Cymen recounts his conversion by the message of the missionary Augustine. The freedom which he discovers from the necessity of sacrifice is valid regardless of whether the pain and payment is inflicted to propitiate the Germanic tribesman's god Woden or the modern secular man's god, himself. Of Augustine's newly delivered message, Cymen says:

> But I have heard
> Word of his God, and felt our lonely flesh
> Welcome to creation. The fearful silence

Became the silence of great sympathy,
The quiet of God and man in the mutual word.
And never again need we sacrifice, on and on
And on, greedy of the gods' goodwill,

or as we in this century might say, greedy of our own goodwill,

But always uncertain; for sacrifice
Can only perfectly be made by God
And sacrifice has so been made, by God
To God in the body of God with man,
On a tree set up at the four crossing roads
Of earth, heaven, time, and eternity
Which meet upon that cross.[26]

The pattern may be diagramed in this way: When man
recognizes his guilt, and is concerned about it, he attempts
to propitiate for himself by giving some sort of sacrificial
service or payment, or by bearing some form of pain. But the
more he attempts to extricate himself, the more deeply he
becomes involved. He hears the Christian claim that atonement and purgation have in fact been made for him, he recognizes that the conditions of the life of Christ reproduce the
archetypal human pattern of atonement approached through
payment and through pain, and by faith he accepts the Christian assurance that the otherwise impossible atonement has
now in fact been made and that his own guilt, which he could
not purge, has now in fact been purged for him.

You may recall that Horace declares it dramatically and
aesthetically false to allow a god to enter the action of a story
unless the action has become so complicated that a resolution
can come in no other way than by the entrance of the god.
And that, declares Martin Luther, is exactly what happened
in the incarnation and atonement: Only God could provide a
denouement to man's complexity, and in Christ, God did
provide it.[27] It is through the recognition of this fact, still in
honesty and in justice, that man finds himself freed from sin

and the burden of guilt. For this reason, the man who in honesty and justice recognizes himself as a sinner can in faith find himself lifted out of the human impasse of sin and guilt into the abundant life of joy through Christ his Savior. The norm and standard of human life is then seen as established, not by death, nor by nature, nor by failure, sin, and guilt, but by the love of God in Christ our Lord.

IV. *Christ and Prometheus*

Perhaps the most essential single thing to understand about the atonement is that Christ is not a Greek Prometheus set opposite an angry god. Any confusion of Christ with Prometheus is both a mark of obtuseness and also the first step toward reducing the incarnation to gibberish and nonsense. Whereas Christ on the cross is wronged by man, Prometheus chained to his rock is wronged by Zeus, against whom he is defiant throughout. The last words of Aeschylus' *Prometheus Bound* are filled with that defiance:

> On me the tempest falls.
> It does not make me tremble.
> O holy Mother Earth, O air and sun,
> Behold me. I am wronged.[28]

There is a nobility in Prometheus' attitude, but there is no reconciliation and no peace, a fact which Aeschylus recognizes, and in a strangely prophetic utterance he has Hermes declare to Prometheus:

> Look for no ending to this agony
> Until a god will freely suffer for you,
> Will take on him your pain, and in your stead
> Descend to where the sun is turned to darkness,
> The black depths of death.
> Take thought: this is no empty boast
> But utter truth.[29]

That hauntingly allusive statement, which comes to Prometheus not as a promise but as a threat, is the closest approach to the Christian incarnation and atonement in Aeschylus' play, and yet it is not a commentary upon what Prometheus either does or can do, but rather upon what needs to be done for him. It is not a prophecy of hope, but rather an assertion of the virtual impossibility of release.

It is then centrally important to remember that Christ is not a Promethean titan painfully opposing a wrathful god. Furthermore, the essential difference between the Christian expiation and the various forms of non-Biblical expiation is precisely in the fact that God's mercy to man is not the result of the expiation but the cause of it: God's mercy is not the result of the cross, but the cause of the cross. The process of redemption cannot be understood by absolutizing the opposition of the Son's love to the Father's anger, for Jesus *is* the Son precisely because he is the fullest possible revelation of the Father. This, after all, is what the incarnation means— not that a heroic man suffered to reconcile an angry god to man, but rather the reverse, that the divine suffered to reconcile angry men to God. "All this," says the apostle Paul, "is from God, who through Christ reconciled us to himself . . . that is, God was in Christ reconciling the world to himself, not counting their trespasses against them."[30]

All of which puts man's situation into an entirely new perspective. A man who as a pre-Christian had only felt guilt and had dimly seen that guilt rooted in one or more particular or general evils, now understands that those evils were not themselves the cause but were the result of an even deeper and more profound evil—existence as his own deity in alienation from God himself. Man's problem is not to be summarized in terms of a list of sins, not even in terms of that remarkably inclusive list of the seven deadly sins, for these sins are themselves the products of a deeply planted originating sin—a phrase which is, I think, more descriptive than original sin—and this originating sin is the creature's will to exist as his own god. The fall of man, by which man has perennially fallen and still falls, is the attempt to establish himself as his own god, and to claim for his own private dominion the fruit of the knowledge of good and evil. Man's assertion of his own deity is not made in terms of the naïve worship of an idol made in his own image, but expresses itself rather in his continual drive to establish himself as the determinative norm of whatever world he inhabits, and to extend the bounds of his habitation so as to extend the determinative power of his own will, bringing persons and things and truth and even God into subjection to himself. It is thus that man repudiates life in the image of God in order to live as god.

That is what is expressed by the Genesis story of the fall of man. Adam, or 'ādhām in the Hebrew, is not a proper name restricted to one man, as you will recall, but a generic noun meaning man, or mankind, and the entire account refers to the total human condition rather than to a chronologically isolated event. It is like one of the New Testament parables told by Christ, not for its accurate delineation of an actual event, but for its accurate insight into all human events. Man's assumption of his own deity is the frail substructure which renders his entire existence unstable, the origin of his alienation from God, from his neighbor, and from himself, and it is this triple alienation which is broken by faith in the action of Christ.

V. *The Delusion of Syncretism*

There is surely nothing new about what I am saying here. It has been said in many ways throughout Christian history, but to my mind even the great theologians have never said

it more effectively than has John Milton in his epic poem
Paradise Lost. In Genesis, the serpent's temptation of Eve was
that she should repudiate the image of God in order to assume deity itself—to "be as gods." Upon this Biblical conception of sin, Milton builds his entire treatment. Thus, in
Paradise Lost, God the Father declares that man's sinful impasse is rooted in "Affecting God-head, and so losing all."
The point is insistently repeated in Satan's temptation of Eve,
as Satan persuades her to "Taste this, and be henceforth
among the Gods, Thyself a Goddess." The reason for repudiating God's commandment, then, is that Eve wills to make
of herself "A Goddess among Gods, ador'd and serv'd." Thus
Man falls by the very assertion of his divinity.[31]

At this point we come upon one of the decisive and irreconcilable differences between the Christian faith and the great
Indian religions. To say this is not to deny the strengths and
beauties of Indian religious achievement, as evidenced in
Hinduism and Buddhism. It is merely to make an empirical
observation of a fact which we should not overlook. In our
own time, many men of good will and high idealism are attempting to achieve a synthesis of world religions, chiefly of
Hinduism or Buddhism with Christianity, and yet their idealism sometimes runs ahead of their powers of observation,
so that the issues are gravely oversimplified and the proposed solutions are as a consequence superficial. Not only
is this true in the very complex and less tangible area of
theological understandings of the divine, but even in the
more directly accessible problem of the nature of man, where
the Hindu and Christian positions directly contradict each
other.

In the Hindu view, man's difficulty is traceable to what is
called original ignorance, or in the Sanskrit, *avidyā,* which is
defined as man's ignorance of his "identity with the Supreme
Being," his failure to recognize that "essentially man is god."[32]

In the Christian view, on the other hand, man's difficulty is original sin, the attempt to attain this very "identity with the Supreme Being," the assumption that "essentially man is God." In this divergence between two views of man we see one irreconcilable difference between the Biblical and the Aryan traditions. These two views simply cannot be merged into one. Here is the clearest case of either/or with which I am familiar in all of human thought. Either man is essentially god, or he is not. Man's difficulty either arises out of his failure to recognize his essential self as identical with the Supreme Being, or it arises out of his presumption of that identity. And his ultimate self-recognition comes either from his recognition that he is at base identical with the Supreme Being or from his recognition that his assertion of that identity is the root of his misery and guilt. We cannot have it both ways. The Hindu view of original ignorance stands in direct contradiction of the Christian view of original sin, and at every crucial point of the teachings of the two religions this original difference in the diagnosis of man's problem finds corresponding differences in the prescriptions advanced for the cure of man's soul.

In *Paradise Lost*, Satan tempts Eve by suggesting to her that she is the victim of original ignorance, and that by eating the fruit of the knowledge of good and evil she will be freed into a larger measure of life, freed, in fact, into divinity, for by eating, he says, "ye should be as Gods," by an act of will "putting off Human, to put on Gods."[33] And it is in precisely these terms that Eve tempts Adam to eradicate his ignorance by participating in this knowledge which, as she says, makes "them Gods who taste."[34] The Christian view of man's condition, then, as conveyed through the parable of the fall, is that man's alienation rests precisely in the point at which Hinduism maintains that his salvation comes. Milton, or the author of Genesis, might indeed have been

presenting Satan's temptation in words paraphrased from
Hindu philosophy, as we find it beautifully summarized in
the words of the Brhād-aranyaka Upaniṣad:

> Whoever knows thus, "I am Brahman" [or the Supreme Being],
> becomes all this. Even the gods cannot prevent his becoming
> thus, for he becomes their self. So whoever worships another
> divinity (than his self) thinking that he is one and (Brahman)
> another, he knows not.[35]

In all dispassionate honesty, intellectual honesty and religious honesty, we must observe that from the perspective of
Christian faith such a view represents the core of original sin,
and conversely we must recognize that from the Hindu (and
derivatively from the Buddhist) perspective the Christian
faith represents the core of original ignorance. We cannot
deride the good intentions of those who in our time are
seeking to synthesize Christianity and the Indian religions
into one great syncretistic world religion. If such a reconciliation were possible, it would surely simplify the religious
situation, as well as the intellectual situation, of man, and
for both reasons it would be a welcome achievement. But, in
view of the facts of the case, syncretism is wishful thinking,
and I cannot see that anything of value is to be achieved by
retiring into such wishful thinking. We must face life as it
is, in honesty, responsibility, and charity, and make the
choices which life forces upon us.

VI. *The Restoration of Man*

Taking the Christian parable of the fall of man, John
Milton interprets its results for Adam and Eve in terms of
a threefold isolation. The first alienation, as we have already
seen, is alienation from God. The second is alienation from

each other. In theory the decision of Adam and Eve to exist as their own deities may sound well enough, but how are gods to live together? Each has claimed deification, each expects to be "ador'd and serv'd,"[36] and conflict is inevitable, as the entire corpus of the Greek mythology of the Olympian gods charmingly demonstrates. Adam and Eve have transformed the parabolic garden of paradise into an Olympus of bickering. Which god is supreme? Which god will give way? Both indulge an individualized knowledge of good and evil by setting themselves up in judgment of each other, each excluding the other from mercy in a contest of mutual recrimination. As Milton puts it,

> Love was not in their looks, either to God
> Or to each other, but apparent guilt,
> And shame, and perturbation, and despair,
> Anger, and obstinacy, and hate, and guile.[37]

Each curses the other away, as both exist in the lonely splendor of hatred and discord:

> Thus they in mutual accusation spent
> The fruitless hours, but neither self-condemning,
> And of their vain contest appear'd no end.[38]

The alienation of Adam from Eve is not an isolated and localized chronological event, but a parabolic incident whose significance cuts across all of human history so long as it is dominated by sin, as Milton clearly points out in his survey of the recurrent antagonism of man to man, class to class, nation to nation, and race to race.

Man's self-chosen deity results not only in antagonism to God and to his fellow men, but also in antagonism to himself. Having repudiated his basic creaturely humanity, he cannot live with his own nature, for he has declared his isolation from it. He therefore judges himself, as well as others, in a

frenzy of self-torture. Here as elsewhere Adam and Eve are
representative figures:

> They sat them down to weep; not only tears
> Rain'd at their eyes, but high winds worse within
> Began to rise, high passions, anger, hate,
> Mistrust, suspicion, discord, and shook sore
> Their inward state of mind, calm region once
> And full of peace, now toss't and turbulent.[39]

The proper self-esteem, which the archangel Gabriel had
taught man he should possess,[40] is now totally lost:

> Just confidence, and native righteousness,
> And honour [were gone] from about them, naked left
> To guilty shame.[41]

The result is what Milton calls "dishonest shame" and "honour dishonourable," a sinful result of sin itself.[42] All things and
all relationships are altered for Adam and Eve. Whereas their
experiences of sexual intercourse before the fall had been
pure and unalloyed in joy, now the "agony of love"[43] enters
in, each using the other as a thing for self-gratification rather
than as a person for mutual fulfillment. Thus they exist, like
the fallen Satan who perverted their peace as well as his own,
in a world

> Where neither joy nor love, but fierce desire,
> Among our other torments not the least,
> Still unfulfill'd with pain of longing pines.[44]

Sleep becomes unrest, anxiety replaces assurance, and the
core of human peace and joy is shattered. Conscience, which
was established as a free inner guide to the end of contentment, has become a thing of torment, as Adam says:

> O Conscience, into what Abyss of fears
> And horrors hast thou driv'n me; out of which
> I find no way, from deep to deeper plung'd.[45]

Man, 'ādhām, here confronts the ultimate human impasse,

and considers the possibility of making his escape by committing suicide or genocide—seeking in this way, as Milton phrases the recurrent theme, "destruction with destruction to destroy."[46] Man recognizes, however, that such a course would not represent contempt for his originating sin, but rather an expansion of it, expressed in "Rancour and pride, impatience and despite, Reluctance against God."[47]

Augustine of Hippo wrote that man is inevitably a slave to the things by which he seeks to be happy, and when man seeks his chief end in himself, he becomes a slave to himself, or, what amounts to the same thing, he is in bondage to sin and death.[48] From that bondage, and from man's fruitless attempts to tunnel a way out of his own perverted existence, God acts to bring release. Of the incarnation and of the atonement by Christ, the archangel Michael tells Adam that

> thy punishment
> He shall endure by coming in the flesh
> To a reproachful life and cursed death,
> Proclaiming Life to all who shall believe
> In his redemption, and that his obedience
> Imputed becomes theirs by Faith, his merits
> To save them, not their own, through legal works.[49]

The act of faith is essential—"his obedience Imputed becomes theirs by Faith"—for man's confidence must be transferred from himself to God. It is only in this way that man finds release from the incessant punishment and pain which in his fallen and necessarily frustrated condition his sin inflicts upon himself and others as he is caught up in the vicious circle of attempting "destruction with destruction to destroy."

The first of man's three alienations, the isolation from God, is overcome for him entirely by the action of God. When the faithful man repudiates the futile attempt to create his own ultimacy, and recognizes that the fullest possibility of exist-

ence is underwritten for him by God, he may then accept
himself as a creature, because God already has accepted him.
The alienation from himself is thus destroyed along with
alienation from God. Having become reconciled to God and
to himself, he can now become reconciled to others, whom
he no longer regards as the rivals of his pretension to ultimacy, as petty deities with whom he must engage in a perpetual re-enactment of Olympian strife. Since his existence
is established by the constant mercy of God, it is no longer at
the fluctuating mercy of human caprice, and man is thus in
a position to accept other men as his brothers rather than as
inevitable threats to his own basic existence. As a result the
life of charity becomes possible, whose purpose is, as Augustine put it, "to enjoy God for his own sake and ourselves
and our neighbor for the sake of God."[50] It is in some such
terms of reconciliation that the universal problem of human
guilt is found to be resolved by those who accept the resolution offered by God in Christ. Man's bondage to the "dark
intolerable inescapable night" to which Oedipus referred is
broken. The human impasse of failure and sin is bridged
over.

With the solution to the universal problem of guilt comes
a solution to the universal problem of human identity. Man,
poised in uncertainty before the possibility of taking the
norm and the standard of his action from a surrounding
nature which he sees to be red in tooth and claw, and the possibility of taking as his norm a human nature which he knows
to be weak and fallible and unable to attain even to its own
ideals, finds the ultimate referent of his being neither in the
divinity of man nor in the goddess of nature but rather in the
incarnate Word of God. The problem of a standard, of a
master pattern by which man may live, is inescapable, and
perennially men try to solve it or to evade it or to fling defiance in its face. In Christopher Fry's *Thor, With Angels,*

Cymen feels it with all the intensity of a passionate nature, torn between the alternatives of grace and human assertion:

> What I'm afflicted with
> Is strong, destroying me with a cry of love,
> A violence of humility arrogantly
> Demanding all I am or possess or have ambitions for,
> Insistent as a tocsin which was sounded
> When the sun first caught on fire, and ever since
> Clangs alarms with a steady beat in the wild
> Night of history. This doesn't come
> From the watery light of what you think you remember.
> A lashing logic drags me away from my gods.
> Let it face me like a man.[51]

To Cymen's demand that the issue face him like a man, Merlin replies by pointing to the figure of Christ:

> It may be already
> This power has faced you like a man, on a certain
> Century's peak from which the circling low land
> Is, to eternity, surveyed.[52]

Man demands a vantage point from which to understand his own existence and history, and this point of vantage is decisively provided for him by Christ, the determinative focal point of human history, through whom man may see his life as a drama with meaning.

And once this has been seen, the remaining one of the three universal human issues with which we were concerned in the preceding chapter is resolved. Man lives in the shadow of death, but that shadow does not destroy the significance of life, does not reduce it to an endless and pointless succession of tomorrows, dragged out like a meaningless tale told by an idiot. It is rather that man can now endure the presence of death in the assurance that the human drama is an action with a meaningful goal, and with the assurance of fulfillment.

Death constitutes a plague to the creature precisely because it denies the creature's assertion of his own ultimacy. So long as the creature persists in the pretense of self-deification, death exacerbates his misery by constantly threatening him with annihilation, and in this way enters into the nexus of evil which is created by sin. Death thus becomes a problem because of the originating sin, although later it creates new problems by its interaction with sin. It is only when sin is overcome, only when man can accept himself as a creature under God rather than as a god among creatures, that death can assume its proper place in relation to life which is a gift of God rather than an inalienable achievement of man.

As God the Father says in *Paradise Lost,* the Son's action gives "Death his death's wound"[53] so that Death is now bound, and man is freed. In the face of the faithful man's assurance that he is freed by Christ, death's power over life is destroyed, and "to the faithful Death [becomes] the Gate of Life."[54] The result again comes not by any human assertion, nor by any intrinsic human immortality. Man's superiority to death is not contingent upon his own powers, but rather upon the merciful supremacy of God. Milton's most dramatic statement of this assurance in *Paradise Lost* is found in the words of God the Father to God the Son:

> at one sling
> Of thy victorious arm, well-pleasing Son,
> Both Sin and Death and yawning Grave at last
> Through Chaos hurl'd, obstruct the mouth of Hell
> Forever, and seal up his ravenous Jaws.[55]

It is not only the final power of death which is thus destroyed, but also the proximate and incessant predation of death upon the meaning and value of daily life, so that man may now recognize himself and his existence as being under the aegis of a God who is like Christ, rather than under the tyranny of a dark and destructive necessity. For Milton's Adam, the result of this recognition is a paean of praise:

> O goodness infinite, goodness immense!
> That all this good of evil shall produce,
> And evil turn to good; more wonderful
> Than that which by creation first brought forth
> Light out of darkness![56]

THE PATTERNS OF CHRISTIAN GROWTH   133

of a clear and destinate re-entity. For Milton's Adam, the
house of his species . . . . of rage

Chapter Five

THE PATTERNS OF
CHRISTIAN GROWTH

I. *Perspective on the Way*

Throughout, these essays on literature and theology have
proposed to be suggestive rather than exhaustive, attempting
to indicate the relevance of certain crucially significant literary instances to the life of men in general and to the life of
Christian men in particular. We began by considering in the
first chapter the manner in which literary methods of parable, metaphor, and dramatic history are basic to Christian
thought. In the second and third chapters we considered the
insights into the universal human situation which great literature provides, insights which clarify both the greatness of the
human potential and the misery and tragic limits of man.
The fourth chapter proceeded to show the manner in which
Christian redemption speaks to the universal problems of
man, so as to open entirely new and radically unique possibilities for human fulfillment through the action of God
in Christ. In that chapter, then, we attempted to explore the
relevance of Christian redemption for the total life of man
as we had previously seen that life developed in literature.

But redemption itself is not the entering of a final gate, to borrow terms from Bunyan's *Pilgrim's Progress;* it is rather the entering of a preliminary gate which puts man on a long road of pilgrimage to the City of God, as the Christian faith gives rise to the Christian life. It is that life—the life of growth in grace—which we will be discussing now, as its temptations, obstacles, and triumphs have been significantly explored and surveyed in literature. A full account of this subject obviously cannot be given in one brief essay, because a full account for English literature alone would have to treat many of the major works of our tradition from the time of the Old English Caedmon and Cynewulf to the present writings of T. S. Eliot, W. H. Auden, and Christopher Fry. All that we can do here is to suggest some of the more significant ways in which the Christian life has been developed in literature.

Since the Christian life involves both life in community and individual life, we must look at these two aspects of Christianity. For the life of community, we will turn primarily to William Langland's medieval allegory *Piers Plowman,* and for the individual life we will consider John Milton's drama *Samson Agonistes.* Of course Langland is also concerned with the individual life, and Milton's poem is throughout implicitly concerned with the life of the people Israel as well as with the life of the man Samson, so that we must recognize that the two aspects of Christian emphasis are never divorced from each other. In Bunyan's *Pilgrim's Progress* we find these two sides of the Christian life clearly displayed in the two parts of the allegory. Part one of *Pilgrim's Progress* deals largely with the individual life of the Christian as he makes his way from the City of Destruction to the City of God, while part two presents the experience of a company of pilgrims traversing the same way together. We have there a stereoscopic view of Christians on pilgrimage, seen individually and collectively. A number of other important points are so clearly considered in *Pilgrim's Progress* that we would do well to begin our consideration with this work. We will then take up *Piers Plowman,* move on from it to a literary exploration of the defection of religion from God, and then turn to *Samson Agonistes* as a treatment of the typical struggles of the man of faith. We will, finally, treat two literary portrayals of heaven as the consummation of everlasting life individually and communally, as these portrayals are found in Dante and in Bunyan.

II. *The Common Way*

At the very outset, however, we must state quite clearly that the mature Christian does not pursue his pilgrimage as though he were taking out a celestial insurance policy, promising gold-paved and eternal annuities. The dominant motive for pilgrimage is the love of God, and Bunyan says of his true pilgrims that they have persevered to the Heavenly City because of "the love that they bear to the King of this place." Heaven is not sought because it is "a palace and state most blessed," but because heaven is the realm of God's love.[1] Recall here that in *Paradise Lost* the demonic prince Mammon had boasted to Satan that his skill could develop in hell a magnificence equal to that of heaven, but Satan nonetheless finds within himself that "which way I fly is Hell; myself am Hell," while his hellish offspring Death declares that "to me . . . Alike is Hell, or Paradise, or Heaven."[2] Metaphorically considered, the "places" heaven and hell are not geographically determined, for in this conception the alienation from God which the damned choose for themselves converts even heaven into a hell for them, as alienation from God is by definition hell. Thus Milton writes of "the hot

Hell" that always burns within Satan though he be "in mid Heav'n," while Satan says of himself that "all good to me becomes Bane, and in Heav'n much worse would be my state."[3]

Within this context it becomes clear that the seeking of a heaven of personal power or gratification or aggrandizement or self-satisfaction is really not seeking heaven at all, but rather seeking hell, as one of Bunyan's pilgrims finds when he is ushered into the bypass to hell at the very gate of heaven. The true motivation for Christian pilgrimage is expressed by another of Bunyan's pilgrims, Christian's young son Samuel, who declares that he goes so that "I may see God, and serve him without weariness; that I may see Christ, and love him everlastingly; that I may have that fulness of the Holy Spirit in me that I can by no means here enjoy." Christian himself makes a statement which is at once broader and simpler when he says that he prefers over the enticements of Apollyon the person, company, and servants of Christ.[4]

That is the mature Christian motivation, and not all of the true Christians in *Pilgrim's Progress* have it at the beginning. Christian himself begins his pilgrimage with a severe feeling of dread and of numinous awe, so that he sets out with less sense of his goal than of his need. His wife, Christiana, however, leaves the City of Destruction because of a specific invitation from the King of Heaven and with a clear sense of favorable destiny and of destination, whereas the young girl Mercy begins her pilgrimage at the invitation of Christiana rather of God. Hopeful sets out because he has been inspired by the martyrdom of Faithful, while Valiant-for-truth leaves because of what appears to be a more intellectual concern for the truth as he says in his straightforward way: "I believed and therefore came out, got into the Way, fought all that set themselves against me, and by believing am come to this Place."[5]

The way of pilgrimage is the same for all the pilgrims, but as the pilgrims themselves differ so do their motivations and so also do their experiences. Thus all Christians must go through the Valley of Humiliation, which Christian finds a terrible trial for his own particularly proud nature, while others not only have no difficulty at this stage of the journey but even find the valley a delightful place. As Mr. Greatheart says, "Here is nothing to hurt us, unless we procure it to ourselves." Similarly, Christian falls into the Slough of Despond, whereas Faithful has no difficulty worth mentioning there; Faithful on the contrary finds himself much tempted by the lusty advances of Mistress Wanton, whereas the purely fleshly sins seem to exert little appeal upon Christian.[6]

Thus Bunyan's great company of clearly individualized pilgrims each has a clearly individual experience of the common way. By his employment of many pilgrims passing over the same way but experiencing it in differing ways, Bunyan provides a fully three-dimensional insight into the life of the Christian and of the Christian church. He gives, as it were, a picture in depth. It is, further, a picture in which there are many allegorical symbols but no stereotypes—for Christian development is not a standardized routine but a highly personal growth in grace.

Like Bunyan's *Pilgrim's Progress,* William Langland's medieval allegory *Piers Plowman* sets all human existence within the frame of the two cities—the City of Destruction and the City of God—as Langland describes the life of the world and the life of the Christian in this world striving to reach the City of God. The title character of Langland's poem is Piers the Plowman, and it is important for us to understand what Piers represents. The name Piers is a medieval form of Peter, whose confession to Jesus that "Thou art the Christ, the son of the living God" is the foundation of the life of the church. And insomuch as he represents Peter, Piers also represents

Christ, since he stands for the true church which as "the body of Christ" continues Christ's work in the world.

Langland's poem opens with a vision of a "fair field full of folk . . . Working and wandering as the world demanded." The folk are at first quite unaware of any need to change their condition, but they become convinced by the allegorical personification Reason that their situation is in fact untenable. Reason, however, cannot show them the way to the new life which they vaguely desire. So the commune prays for guidance "that Grace might go with them to seek Truth,"[7] and shortly thereafter two new figures appear, between whom the people must decide as to which represents the true guide to the City of Truth.

First there comes an experienced and seemingly authoritative pilgrim, described as the perfect model of what medieval men thought of as the wayfarer to shrines and holy places:

> An hundred ampules hung at his hatband,
> Signs from Sinai and shells from Galice,
> Many a cross on his cloak, and keys from Rome,
> And the vernicle in front, that friends might find it,
> And see by his signs what shrines he had been to.[8]

The folk inquire as to where he has been, and he confidently answers that he has been to Sinai and Bethlehem and the holy sepulcher and has "sought good saints for my soul's welfare."[9] Translated into twentieth-century terms, it is as though the pilgrim were to say that he had studied at a currently fashionable theological seminary, that he had then proceeded beyond his initial degrees to take graduate work under Bultmann, Tillich, and Barth, and finally that he had a long list of published books and articles to his credit. Surely such a man must know the way to God, the people feel, and so they ask his guidance:

> "Know you aught of a Saint whom men call Truth?"

> Can you put us on the path to the place where he is
>   dwelling?"[10]

Essentially, the question is, Do you know God and the way
to heaven? The perennial seeker replies as if shocked:

> "No, so God help me!" said this great traveller,
> "I never saw a palmer, with pike and wallet,
> Ask after him before, till now, at this moment."[11]

It is precisely at this point of crisis that Piers the Plowman
appears to declare to the commune of man's pilgrimage to
Truth that

> if you wish to know the way to his manor,
> I shall put you on the path to the place where he is dwelling.[12]

Piers' arrival upon the scene is dramatic, as it should be if it
is to be in keeping with the importance of his role. But
though his entry is dramatic, it is not cataclysmic. It is even
muted, for the character of Piers is of far more importance
than is at once apparent. Thus Piers' entry, though decisive
for the larger action of the poem, is inconclusive and unin-
spiring for many of the folk. One professional clergyman
denies outright the validity of Piers' program, another insults him for a fool, and many of the people refuse to accept
his leadership, following instead such guidance as they may
find from a thief, a pardoner, a prostitute, or a peddler.[13] The
lure of visible and attainable goods, the availability for a price
of assurance for the future along with pleasure and food for
the present appear far more attractive than the hard course
which Piers discloses.

But Piers himself is undaunted. His first description of the
road to God is full and rich in allegorical meaning. Going
through Meekness, he says, the pilgrim must continue to Conscience until Christ knows that he loves God above all things
and his neighbor next. He must proceed by way of the
Decalogue until he arrives at Truth's castle, which is de-

fended only by a moat of mercy and by walls made of true wisdom buttressed with belief. The divine castle is roofed with Love and Low-Speech-of-Brethren, while the supporting pillars are made of penance and the prayers of saints, and the gates swing open and shut upon hinges of almsdeeds.

No one can enter God's castle except by the action of Grace, the gatekeeper, who guards the entrance with his assistant Amend-you. The passwords are the honest affirmations of repentance, and the pilgrim after giving these may bid Amend-you in reliance upon his master Grace to "raise up" the wicket gate that Eve shut, and Grace will then open the gate freely in response to the pilgrim's earnest desire. Thereupon, man will not only enter the dwelling place of Truth but will find that Truth simultaneously establishes a dwelling place in the human personality:

> And if Grace grant you to go in freely,
> You shall see in yourself Truth in your heart's chamber,
> In a chain of charity and a child's likeness
> To suffer and to say nothing against your Sire's wishes.[14]

The pilgrim is warned by Piers, moreover, to beware lest "pride to praise your own merits" mount up in envy of God even in the last stages of the journey, and "so you may lose His love from liking yourself better."[15]

Having outlined the course of the pilgrimage to the City of God, however, Piers now turns decisively to other considerations in which the sturdy this-worldliness of Christianity comes to the fore, as Piers declines to lead a pilgrimage on the quest for salvation until the full communal implications of the Christian evangel are recognized and accepted. So he declares that he has "half an acre to harrow by the highway" before he can set the pilgrimage on its way. This earthy half acre is crucially important. Until it is attended to, there can be no movement to the celestial city. To it the final cantos of the first major section of the poem are devoted, and here the Christian is lessoned in being God's "pilgrim at the plow,"[16] working upon the earth with its most earthy substance in co-operation with his brothers for the benefit of the human community before seeking entrance at the gate of heaven. No image could more forcefully impel a recognition of the futility of mere otherworldliness.

The plowing is no easy task; there is defection and malingering, but Truth commands Piers to continue working the ground. Against the background of society's greedy huckstering and consumption, Piers' program for the half acre represents a system of love which would totally reorder the entire life of the fair field. As devotion to the world and time corrupts the world and time, so devotion to heaven and the everlasting will transform the earthly and the temporal.

So Piers, under Truth, teaches and desires, but the defections continue. A professional churchman significantly speaks out in ridicule of Piers, calls him a fool, and totally misses his identity as the true church. "Rude rogue," Piers says to him, "you have read little in the Bible."[17]

The struggle between the true church as the body of Christ and the corruption of laity, clergy, friars, and prelates gathers force through most of *Piers Plowman,* until in the concluding cantos the small and faithful remnant is continuously opposed by the "Company of Comfort,"[18] a medieval version of modern cults of oversimplified peace of mind and peace of soul, who find in easy confession and easy penance a softer balm than the balm of Gilead. The faithful parson now seems to be too severe in the cure of sin:

> The plasters and powders of the parson bite sorely.
> He lets them lie overlong, and is loath to change them.
> From Lent to Lent he lets his plasters bite.[19]

Successful clergymen, on the other hand, supply men with "a glass helmet" against the blows of Age,[20] and with them the

Company of Comfort increases in numbers until it usurps upon the church, with easy confessors and shrift without pain. The process of defection is symbolized in the person of Friar Flattery, who

> crept and gathered and glossed over his shriving,
> Till Contrition had forgotten his crying and weeping,
> And waking for his wickedness, as he was wont formerly.
> For this comfortable confessor he left contrition wholly,
> Which is the sovereign salve for all our sins.[21]

In terms of such a bland view of sin, there is really no need for contrition, and with the loss of contrition, the soul's battle is lost. It is only through Contrition and Confession that man begins his outreach toward God's castle, as God offers his hand to man through the incarnation. Man's action, God's action—and the two must join if the pilgrimage is to be completed. God made clear the larger outcome of the war for man's salvation when in the joust at Jerusalem Christ cleared the highway for those who would make the pilgrimage under Grace. It remained for man to take the road which was thus cleared. But man refuses, and man's society refuses, as man, church, and commune accept the devices of Antichrist in pride and a flattering view of sin. God has fought as man's champion and has offered him victory in the great war, but man all too often achieves his own defeat in the remaining battles.

III. *The Pretense of Growth*

The defections to which Langland refers in the visible church are a continual threat to man's pilgrimage, for each in some way diverts attention from the true course of human redemption and focuses attention instead upon some false hope born of pride or self-interest. In varied ways, the church repeatedly makes an idol of itself or of its sacraments or of its hierarchy or of its message or of its form of doctrine, and worships the creature instead of the Creator, so that it repeatedly performs what Milton treats as the usurpation upon the Holy Spirit:

> What will they then
> But force the Spirit of Grace itself, and bind
> His consort Liberty?[22]

The dangerous thing about Antichrist is not to be found in the fact of his radical difference from Christ but rather in the fact that this radical difference is cloaked under an apparent similarity, so that the Antichrist attempts to destroy the work of Christ while seeming to advance it. One of the most striking things about the dragon-slaying St. George in Edmund Spenser's *The Faerie Queene* is that while St. George defeats the dragons, as palpable symbols of evil, he is himself thoroughly and disastrously duped by a kindly old man in ministerial garb and a lovely young lady in distress, a couple representing the interests of the Antichrist and the whore of Babylon. Apparent piety, or purity, is far more deceptive than open evil and, as Old Testament prophets and Christian poets have repeatedly emphasized, the righteous life of faith may find that the greatest temptations are presented in religious guise. Dante is adamant on this point, as he repeatedly attacks defections within the church. He writes in *The Divine Comedy* that the temple of God is invaded by hucksters, the abbeys are a great den of thieves, and the pope brews a "plot, where daily Christ is sold and bought."[23] Denouncing apostate preachers who confuse the issues of salvation with "fond inventions" irrelevant to the gospel or even contrary to it, Dante declares that Christ did not give as a missionary commandment the preaching of trifles or the telling of jokes:

> Now they go forth to preach with quip and quirk,
>   And if a good laugh they contrive to win,
>   The puffed hood covers a contented smirk.[24]

The sheep are fed with nothing but wind, and when we read Dante's repeated attacks upon the corruption of the medieval church we cannot fail to recall the similar denunciations by John Milton of an established post-Reformation clergy whose

> lean and flashy songs
> Grate on their scrannel pipes of wretched straw.
> The hungry sheep look up, and are not fed,
> But swoln with wind, and the rank mist they draw,
> Rot inwardly, and foul contagion spread.[25]

Like Old Testament prophets, Dante and Langland, Spenser and Milton, denounce the apostasy of religion from God, and Dante even goes so far as to put into the mouth of St. Peter in paradise the assertion that the papacy is vacant and the succession broken. The pope whom Dante thus deposes is Boniface VIII, the same who had declared that by virtue of his office he could judge all men, and could be judged by none. But Dante nonetheless judges him—he has already prepared a place for him in hell—in these words spoken by Peter:

> He who the place usurpeth that was mine
>   On earth, mine, mine, now vacant in the sight
>   Of the Son of God, has made my grave decline
> Into a sewer, well-nigh choked outright
>   With blood and filth: wherein the Arch-Renegade,
>   Who fell from here, down there taketh delight.[26]

We find, too, in Bunyan's *Pilgrim's Progress* that the most effective temptations presented to the wayfaring Christian are not those which would lead him to turn decisively away from God, but are rather those which deceptively present a seemingly easier way to reach God than the way which God has in fact provided.

The situation is perennial, and may be illustrated in any age. In our own time, literature offers many instances of the deceptive guides who present themselves to would-be pilgrims. Carl Sandburg, in his free verse poem "To a Contemporary Bunkshooter," addresses himself to the fundamentalist street preacher who converts the redemptive message of grace into a new and maddening legalism. Sandburg says to the preacher:

> I've read Jesus' words. I know what he said. You don't
> throw any scare into me. I've got your number. I
> know how much you know about Jesus. . . .
> When are you going to quit making the carpenters build
> emergency hospitals for women and girls driven crazy
> with wrecked nerves from your gibberish about Jesus—
> I put it to you again: Where do you get that stuff;
> what do you know about Jesus?[27]

Or, for the other side of the social coin, there is the fashionable Fifth Avenue church described by Eugene O'Neill. As the church lets out on Sunday morning, the parishioners are discussing the marvelous sermon of their minister who is named, quite significantly, Doctor Caiaphas. O'Neill presents the conversation in this way:

> "Dear Doctor Caiaphas! He is so sincere!"
> "What was the sermon? I dozed off."
> "About the radicals, my dear—and the false doctrines that
> are being preached.
> We must organize a hundred per cent American bazaar.
> And let everyone contribute one one-hundredth per cent of
> their income tax."
> "What an original idea!"
> "We can devote the proceeds to rehabilitating the veil of the
> temple."[28]

George Bernard Shaw sums up the case against using any
church body as an instrument for social conformity in one
of his frequent attacks upon the Anglican establishment when
he writes that

> the Church of England itself is compelled to add to the thirty-
> six articles in which it formulates its religious tenets, three more
> in which it apologetically protests that the moment any of
> these articles comes in conflict with the State it is to be en-
> tirely renounced, abjured, violated, abrogated and abhorred,
> the policeman being a much more important person than any
> Person of the Trinity.[29]

In addition to the perils of an Erastian conformity in religion, there are also the perils of the kind of popular piety
which is so often associated in our culture with a commercial
Christmas. In *The Catcher in the Rye,* J. D. Salinger has
given us a memorable description of New York's famous
Radio City Christmas pageant as seen through the eyes of
his teen-aged hero:

> Then they had this Christmas thing they have at Radio City
> every year. All these angels start coming out of boxes and
> everywhere, guys carrying crucifixes and stuff all over the place,
> and the whole bunch of them—*thousands* of them—singing
> "Come All Ye Faithful!" like mad. Big deal. It's supposed to
> be religious as hell, I know, and very pretty and all, but I
> can't see anything religious or pretty, for God's sake, about a
> bunch of actors carrying crucifixes all over the stage.[30]

And we must not omit Peter de Vries' portrayal of that
perfect hyperliberal clergyman the Reverend Andrew Mackerel who holds that it is impossible to write a sermon "fit for
civilized consumption" while faced with the assertion that
Jesus saves.[31] Mackerel's church is called "People's Liberal"
and proudly boasts that it is "the first split-level church in
America. . . . Thus People's Liberal is a church designed

to meet the needs of today, and to serve the whole man. This includes the worship of a God free of outmoded theological definitions and palatable to a mind come of age in the era of Relativity." Among Mackerel's sermons, his own favorite proclaimed that "it is the final proof of God's omnipotence that he need not exist in order to save us," an idea which so delighted his fashionable Connecticut congregation that "he was given an immediate hike in pay and invited out to more dinners than he could possibly eat."[32]

And then in Tennessee Williams' *Cat on a Hot Tin Roof* there is "Reverend Tooker," parson of St. Paul's in Grenada. "His head slightly, playfully, fatuously cocked, with a practiced clergyman's smile, sincere as a bird-call blown on a hunter's whistle, the living embodiment of the pious, conventional lie," this sociable clergyman moves in and out through one of the families of his congregation, a family which is plagued with hatred, suspicion, lust, greed, perversion, and death. Through all of this, Tooker talks only of the need for building up the church, by which he means the need for improving the physical plant and for new stained glass, but he has nothing whatsoever to say which is of any value to the tortured people of that family. As soon as the volcano of its human emotions bursts out into violent conflict and catastrophe, the clergyman hastily excuses himself and departs at once, thus underscoring the total irrelevance of his brand of religion to any real human crisis.[33]

But for a summation of churchly defections in our time we could scarcely do better than to turn to the "Letters of Ghostly Wit" entitled *From a Christian Ghetto*, written by that remarkably versatile Scots clergyman and philosopher, Geddes MacGregor. Much of twentieth-century churchmanship is based, MacGregor holds, on the fatuous assumption that what is needed to convert the world is a cheap aura of respectable good fellowship, "a discreetly hearty handshake with the Right Hand of Fellowship wielded from the elbow."[34] Particularly effective is MacGregor's description of a typical Sunday morning service conducted according to the rites of what he has called "Orthodox pretend-Christianity." As the narrator of the story enters the sanctuary a few minutes before eleven he is alarmed by the uproar of the congregation which he fears is a prelude to violent controversy, but which he soon learns is only "a little chit-chat to preclude the possibility of taking anything too seriously." He sits down, and the service begins, without, however, interfering with the chit-chat.

> The lady on my right had been chattering to me till I was afraid the imitation cherries would fall off her hat. She kept telling me how very much she welcomed me to the midst, as she put it, and explained how important she thought it was for visitors to the temple to get a hearty welcome, because otherwise they mightn't get what she called "the experience" and would go away without having pretended anything at all.[35]

And then comes the clergyman's prayer:

> O dear, wonderful Father of our incredibly unbelievable experience, we like to feel assured that we may always come to thee when we feel like it. . . . And now, dear Lord, we want quite naturally and simply and just in a word to ask thee, very frankly, to give us our heart's desire. Thou art the Comforter, as the old story puts it, and so thou art our friend, for we are very fond of comfort.[36]

The service is concluded with the morning sermon, which proclaims neither good news nor bad but is "just a nice little talk that might perhaps be able to help some people to feel better."[37]

So, in our own age as in every age, we see the manifold subversion of the Christian mission. Langland's Company of

Comfort, Dante's joke-preaching comic friars, Milton's followers of wind and rank mist, all have their counterparts in
our time, and we cannot summarize the entire tragic defection better than by again recalling the fact that Bunyan in
his *Pilgrim's Progress* places an entrance to hell at the very
gates of heaven.

IV. *The Individual Struggle*

But despite all the deceptive enticements to turn aside, the
way itself is open, and the faithful pilgrims who enter through
the door of Christ may persist until they arrive at the City
of God, as Bunyan makes clear in his verse description of
Valiant-for-truth:

> Who would true valour see,
> Let him come hither;
> One here will constant be,
> Come wind, come weather.
> There's no discouragement,
> Shall make him once relent
> His first avow'd intent,
> To be a pilgrim.[38]

In treating the Christian life, we could do no better than
to study Bunyan's *Pilgrim's Progress* in detail, but that is
too large a task for one short chapter,[39] and so I suggest that
we look instead to Milton's *Samson Agonistes,* which is briefer
in scope but has great stature in its own right. Milton adopted
the interpretation of Samson as a type of the man of faith,
an interpretation established by the Epistle to the Hebrews
and developed through the Christian tradition until in Milton's time it was possible for Samson to represent the typical
struggles of the typical Christian life. Milton thus entitles his
poem *Samson Agonistes,* or Samson in *agon,* engaged in the

struggles of the holy war. Then, too, by setting these struggles within the literary form of classical Greek tragedy, Milton implies the identity of the problems which all men face, as well as the uniqueness of the Biblical resolution to those problems.

Milton's dramatic poem opens upon Samson, blind and in chains, bound like an ox at the mill in Gaza where he must grind out his enemies' grain in the torture of his own degradation. Having once walked the earth "like a petty god" "swoll'n with pride," Samson now finds himself shut up within his own prison, without hope of escape by his own efforts. He thus becomes a symbol of the universal state of man, and we recall both the experience and the expression of Oedipus when Samson speaks in despair of his own situation:

> O dark, dark, dark, amid the blaze of noon,
> Irrecoverably dark, total eclipse,
> Without all hope of day. . . .
> As in the land of darkness yet in light,
> To live a life half dead, a living death,
> And buried; but O yet more miserable,
> Myself my sepulchre, a moving grave![40]

But out of this very despair and out of the dreadful consciousness that he has brought dishonor and obloquy to the cause of God and God's people, Samson's reviving hope comes in that he now sees the outcome of the holy war as being entirely in the hands of God himself and not at all in his own hands of pride. So pride gives way to faith that God will win the contest with the Philistinian idol Dagon:

> This only hope relieves me, that the strife
> With me hath end; all the contest is now
> 'Twixt God and Dagon.[41]

The way to God, which Samson's defection seems to have closed, will thus be reopened by the action of God himself, and it is this faith and hope which sustains Samson despite the fact that he does not yet even vaguely suspect that he will himself be the instrument by which that victory is won.

What he has now done is significant precisely because he no longer puts himself into the center of the action, as though everything depended upon himself. He thus repudiates the earlier "petty god" view of his own importance, but there are still opportunities for him to make new defections from the way upon which he is now embarked. Although no mere diagram can exhaust man's seemingly limitless capacity for evil, there is a useful set of categories available in the New Testament reference to the lust of the eyes, the lust of the flesh, and the pride of life, or the world, the flesh, and the devil. The first represents the temptation which comes to each person to warp his own divinely established individuality into conformity with the debased and debasing image accepted by the particular world in which he lives; the second suggests the temptation that man accept as his chief end his own physical and material comfort; while the last suggests the temptation which everyone feels to exalt himself, whether in the pride of pomp or in the pride of humility, above God and God's will for his life. Each of these temptations is presented to Samson in such a fashion as could lead him to abandon his vocation and chief end. And the same temptations which apply to Samson as the faithful man can also apply in any age to the individual man of faith or to the church as the community of faith.

The first temptation is presented by Samson's well-meaning father Manoa, who urges him to come to terms with the world as it is. Manoa would have Samson make a bond with the Philistines, by which he would be released from prison and could devote himself to appeasing God by religious offerings and ritual observances. The case which Manoa makes is a plausible one: there is nothing which Samson can now do to alter the dominant state of society, and so he must look about, see the way things are, and come to terms with reality, evil though it is. It is the counsel of a kind but worldly wisdom: bow to necessity, make your peace, come to terms, abandon the earthly struggle, and engage yourself in the established exercises of religious devotion. But blind and tortured though he is, Samson refuses to sanction the *status quo* even though he has no prospect whatsoever of changing it. His refusal of the temptation of the world is in no sense based upon hope—"Nor am I in the list of them that hope,"[42] he says. His condition may better be described as a faithful despair, in which his only hope for himself is the hope of death:

> This one prayer yet remains, might I be heard,
> No long petition, speedy death,
> The close of all my miseries, and the balm.[43]

The second temptation, that of the flesh, is presented to Samson by Dalila, the Philistine wife who had betrayed him and who now comes to ask his forgiveness and to persuade him that he should return to live with her. She loves him, she says, and would set him free from enforced labor, so that she might appease his loss of sight by every amends within her power. She promises him a life of ease, filled with comfort, luxury, and pleasure, as she pleads that it would be foolhardy of him not to accept and to enjoy such a life as she may provide for him:

> though sight be lost,
> Life yet hath many solaces, enjoy'd
> Where other senses want not their delights
> At home in leisure and domestic ease,
> Exempt from many a care and chance.[44]

In effect Dalila suggests that Samson has no better hope than to devote himself to enjoying the life of the flesh, beyond

which nothing remains to him. But Samson refuses, holding
that there is more freedom for him even in prison than there
would be in a life dedicated only to such self-gratification:

> This gaol I count the house of liberty
> To thine, whose doors my feet shall never enter.[45]

The two temptations thus far presented to Samson have
not sought to discredit his divine vocation as such: they have
merely assumed that his appointed role is now impossible
and that he should as a result either come to terms with the
world as Manoa suggests or seek his gratification in the flesh
and its comforts as Dalila proposes. The final temptation,
however, makes a direct assault upon Samson's sense of identity and of vocation. This is the temptation of Harapha, a
Philistine giant who comes to taunt and humiliate Samson,
and even worse to discredit the very foundation of his life as
a man of faith by asserting that at best his religion was only
primitive magic, that his claim to be the champion of a
chosen people was really a deception cloaking robbery and
pillage, and that in the final analysis God has no interest in
him or care for him, but has discarded him as a thing useless
and outworn.

Here, then, is the most dangerous assault of the demonic
powers, for Samson is attacked at the very point where he is
weakest. If he replies to Harapha's taunts of his worthlessness
by asserting for himself his own worthiness, then he has fallen
into the devil's own trap, for he has exalted himself in pride
and so is lost. On the other hand, if he repudiates himself as
being utterly worthless, in the terms which the demonic
appraisal suggests, then he will have given himself up and so
will be lost in still another sense.

The final temptation of Samson is also the final temptation
which, in *Pilgrim's Progress*, Apollyon proposes to the wayfaring Christian in the Valley of Humiliation, when he ac-
cuses him of being a worthless fellow, repeatedly failing to

live up to his own declared aspirations and throughout
plagued by pride, for as Apollyon says "thou art inwardly
desirous of vainglory in all that thou sayest or doest."[46] Here
even the devil speaks true, for the accusation is based upon
observation of the patent facts and will perennially be advanced against the Christian and against the Christian church.
Both individual and community are continually tempted to
yield to the demonic either by admitting the demonic appraisal of their own worthlessness in the nihilism which is
damnation or by making a demonic assertion of their own
ultimacy and so achieving damnation in that way.

Both Bunyan's Christian and Milton's Samson admit the
charges of their own defection, but they refuse to concede
that their admitted sinfulness is the final word on their being.
They accept, instead, the appraisal which is placed upon
them in mercy by the grace of God. "All of this is true,"
Christian replies to Apollyon, "and much more, which thou
hast left out; but the Prince whom I serve and honour is merciful, and ready to forgive."[47] Samson replies to Harapha in
similar terms:

> All these indignities, for such they are
> From thine, these evils I deserve and more,
> Acknowledge them from God inflicted on me
> Justly, yet despair not of his final pardon
> Whose ear is ever open, and his eye
> Gracious to readmit the suppliant;
> In confidence whereof I once again
> Defy thee to the trial of mortal fight,
> By combat to decide whose god is God,
> Thine or whom I with Israel's sons adore.[48]

The trial by combat suggested here is not a merely roman-
tic survival of primitive chivalry which Milton has introduced
to enliven his action, but is an intensely meaningful symbol
by which Milton conveys the fact that a man really stakes
his life, his entire existence, upon his decision as to "whose

god is God." Samson is very clear as to the issues which are
really involved here, and consistently refuses to allow Harapha to lead him into an obfuscating debate over peripheral
matters. Thus Samson returns again and again to the challenge of mortal combat as he seeks to remove the matter from
the level of fashionable taunting and inject it with ultimate
concern. Although Harapha refuses the challenge and prefers
to keep the conflict within the safer bounds of a dialectic
which merely counterfeits the existential conflict, the result
of the encounter for Samson is that his spirit revives, and
Harapha who had come to reduce Samson to the base point
of humiliation actually offers the stimulus by which he is
revitalized and renewed. In the encounter with Harapha,
Samson has met and overcome the last of the three crucial
temptations, as the Chorus says in summary of his life,

> With God not parted from him, as was fear'd,
> But favouring and assisting to the end.[49]

By winning the internal victory over three crucial temptations to abandon his vocation under God, Samson has now
been prepared for winning the climactic external victory
against the enemies of God's people. The final act of Milton's
drama stirringly recounts that victory.

After Harapha's departure a Philistine officer comes to
order Samson's attendance upon the festival at which his
enemies are celebrating the defeat and degradation of his
people. At first Samson refuses, but then a new possibility
vaguely presents itself to his mind and he agrees to go with
the officer and give an exhibition of his strength before the
Philistine assembly. To the Chorus of Israelites he says:

> Be of good courage; I begin to feel
> Some rousing motions in me which dispose
> To something extraordinary my thoughts.[50]

With Samson gone, Manoa and the Chorus discuss what

can be done for him and what will become of him, plotting what they might practicably do to ransom him from his captors and dreaming of what God might miraculously do to restore his lost sight. There is a touching irony in both hopes, for while they are considering what they can do in the interests of Samson, they hear the devastating sound of what Samson has already done in the cause of God and of his people. First comes the sound of a "universal groan As if the whole habitation perish'd,"[51] and then a messenger arrives to report that Samson has brought down the building upon himself and upon the Philistine enemies of his people, achieving in his death the mission of his life. In the epilogue of the chorus we find Milton's final poetic comment upon the life of faith, with its trials and temptations, defeats and victories:

> All is best, though oft we doubt,
> What th' unsearchable dispose
> Of highest wisdom brings about,
> And ever best found in the close.
> Oft he seems to hide his face,
> But unexpectedly returns
> And to his faithful champion hath in place
> Bore witness gloriously; whence Gaza mourns
> And all that band them to resist
> His uncontrollable intent;
> His servants he with new acquist
> Of true experience from this great event
> With peace and consolation hath dismiss'd,
> And calm of mind, all passion spent.[52]

V. *The Heavenly City*

Now Samson's triumph is neither a merely personal victory nor a merely national one, underscoring the prowess of an epic hero. We must remember that the Philistines represent not only a physical enemy, but even more importantly represent the forces which prevent the people of God from entering into full possession of the Land of Promise, and so stand symbolically for everything which blocks the pilgrim in his quest for the "city which hath foundations, whose builder and maker is God."[53] To draw a parallel with Bunyan, the Philistines may be compared to everything in the way of giants, monsters, and deceivers which seek to prevent the Christians of *Pilgrim's Progress* from reaching the Heavenly City. All of this is present at least by implication in the selection of Samson as a type of faith in the Epistle to the Hebrews. It serves as a subtle ideational basis for Milton's *Samson Agonistes,* and we must keep it clearly in mind in order to understand the full implications of Samson's destruction of the Philistine assembly. Samson's act represents a personal triumph, but it also represents the triumph of the faithful community. By it, the entire people of God are enfranchised for the full possession of the Land of Promise, as Samson's own heroism is caught up into the redeeming grace of God.

As we observed early in this chapter, the human personality can find its full expression only in the presence of God in everlasting life. For the Christian tradition, the Land of Promise symbolically points toward the life everlasting, in which man will realize his fullest potential. Thus the human personality is not merged into an absolute so as to lose personal identity in the divine vastness, after the conception of ultimate release which we find in the traditional Indian religions. But at the same time, the Christian symbols point also to the conviction that the life of the redeemed is life in a community, and not the life of a set of isolated and eternal hermits. You will recall that in *Paradise Lost,* Milton treats the results of sin as a threefold isolation whereby the sinner is alienated from God, from himself, and from his neighbor.

You will recall also that the process of redemption breaks down the partitioning walls of each of these isolations, so that man can love, accept, and enjoy God, his neighbor, and himself. That process, which is begun on earth, is consummated in the life everlasting. Man can exist as a fully developed human being only in terms of such a life, lived in the divine presence, in the communion of saints, in the City of God. If he is to find ultimate fulfillment for his existence, he can do so only there.

But the City of God is a realm which has always presented the greatest difficulty for Christian poets and theologians. Men of every age both within and without the church have by the nature of things been more conversant with the conditions of sin and misery than with the fullest measures of beatitude, for sin is native to the present area of life as an experience of heaven is not. Furthermore, the church militant knows the earthly means of grace and growth in grace from experiences both past and present, but only the church triumphant knows the life of heaven. Thus the life everlasting can never be presented in blueprint, but, as we have seen the great Christian poets and theologians insisting, only in terms of suggestive metaphors, parables, and symbols.

The Christian attitude toward the life everlasting can, I suspect, scarcely be better summarized than in the words of Mr. Stand-fast in *Pilgrim's Progress,* as he prepares to enter the heavenly city:

> I have formerly lived by hear-say and faith, but now I go where I shall live by sight, and shall be with Him in whose company I delight myself.[54]

There is, in that, nothing whatsoever of crassness or vulgarity, nothing of an egocentric desire for self-enjoyment, but an entire devotion to God united with desire to live in his presence. And for the act of departing this life in that devo-

tion there is Bunyan's description of the manner in which
Mr. Valiant-for-truth crosses the river of death:

> And then it was noised abroad that Mr. Valiant-for-truth was
> taken with a summons. . . . When he understood it, he called
> for his friends and told them of it. Then said he, "I am go-
> ing to my fathers, and though with great difficulty I am got
> hither, yet now I do not repent me of all the trouble I have
> been at to arrive where I am. My sword, I give to him that
> shall succeed me in my pilgrimage, and my courage and skill,
> to him that can get it. My marks and scars I carry with me, to
> be a witness for me that I have fought his battles who will now
> be my rewarder." When the day that he must go hence was
> come, many accompanied him to the river side, into which as
> he went he said, "Death, where is thy sting?" And as he went
> down deeper he said, "Grave, where is thy victory?" So he
> passed over, and the trumpets sounded for him on the other
> side.[55]

The trumpets sounding on the other side serve as a master-
ful symbol of the communal joy of heaven, by which all are
delighted with the arrival of new additions to the hosts of
the redeemed in Bunyan's City of God. In Dante's *Divine
Comedy,* the most striking single difference between hell and
heaven is found in the fact that hell is the seat of pride and
hatred, and therefore of an essential and unbridgeable isolation in misery, whereas heaven is the seat of love, and therefore of community in joy. In the *Paradise,* the arrival of each
new individual increases joy, as there are more persons toward whom charity may be directed. Thus the radical dis-
tinctiveness of personalities in heaven, far from developing
discord and rivalry, actually produces love and contentment,
so that it is only here that there is complete individuality *and*
complete community. Each of the redeemed loves God above
all else, and all now recognize without question God's love
for themselves, so that they now enjoy the only true security

which allows them to love each other and themselves in a total community of joy. Such a life cannot and, as Dante puts it,

> is not to be shown
> To the eyes of him whose unperfected wit
> Hath not in love's flame into ripeness grown.[56]

In the highest heaven of pure light, understanding and love are inextricably connected:

> Light of the understanding, full of love,
> Love of the true good, full of joy within,
> Joy that transcends all the heart conceiveth of.[57]

The joy which is repeatedly underscored in the *Paradise* is not an end in itself, but is rather a by-product stemming from the total acceptance of God, which is man's chief end. Similarly, as the only ultimate fulfillment of personality comes in terms of accepting the ultimacy of God, rather than of the self or of its egocentric "joy," so in a similar way the only ultimate synthesis comes rather in terms of love than of definition. Thus when Dante comes in the *Paradise* to the direct vision of "the Love that moves the sun and the other stars," he finds that this Love binds together "in one volume the scattered leaves of all the universe." Here, then, we see the reuniting in an image of synthesis of all the disjointed and seemingly meaningless fragments of life, the constitution of a now intelligible wholeness in the circle of the divine trinity in unity, represented by a "sublime light, which in itself is true."[58] And the "synthesis" thus achieved is primarily a synthesis of love. God is now seen face to face as pure, profound, unbounded light, in the contemplation of whom the utmost potential of the human personality is realized, as the "mind a sudden glory assailed And its wish came revealed to it in that light."[59] Language is strained to the breaking point, and still the human imagination cannot express the experience of God:

> To the high imagination force now failed;
>   But like to a wheel whose circling nothing jars,
>   Already on my desire and will prevailed
> The Love that moves the sun and other stars.[60]

Epilogue

EPILOGUE

Dante's epic closes in the City of God, where human individuality and human community find consummation in the presence of Father, Son, and Holy Spirit, and of the faithful of all ages. It is useless to ask that this vision be translated into either literal or abstract terms, for Dante's method is literary, and the literary can be reduced neither to a merely literalistic nor to a merely statemental plane. It has its own integrity—not the smaller integrity of verisimilitude, but the larger integrity of veracity.

As with Dante, so elsewhere, it is in such terms that the Christian humanist will understand the great Christian literary classics. And it is in these terms, too, that he will approach the Christian Scriptures upon which those classics are based, interpreting the Scriptural accounts in terms of an understanding of dramatic history which at once preserves inviolable the integrity of historical events and of the distinctively literary means by which those events are communicated. The Word became flesh in history for man's redemption, but for that historical redemption to be made available to successive generations the Word incarnate in history is borne by the words of literary communication to men far removed in time and place from the original happenings.

The Christian also finds insights into God's will through nonhistoric materials, as metaphor, symbol, and parable adapt ultimate truths to proximate reality in terms accommodated to man's understanding. It is for all these reasons that Luther's assertion still carries force—that "without knowledge of literature pure theology cannot at all endure." In our own time the Scriptures are distorted by unbalanced assertions both of the left and the right. Against such distortion, the kind of Christian humanism to which I am referring provides a balanced and viable alternative. Indeed, one great prerequisite for extending the genuine influence of the Scriptures in our own time, as in the time of the Reformation, is that men should approach the Scriptures in terms of literary understanding for by this, "as by no other means," Luther tells us, "people are wonderfully fitted for the grasping of sacred truth and for handling it skillfully and happily."

But more is involved than method. It is in literature, as nowhere else, that the human condition is laid bare, that man is made known to himself in all his greatness and in all his misery. Nowhere better than in literature do we understand the tremendous human achievement of ordering existence through compassion, understanding, and beauty. And nowhere do we so graphically encounter the limits of man, as his powers exhaust themselves and he stands perplexed and helpless before the ultimate problems of death, identity, and guilt. Man comes to Christianity out of human experience, and though Christian redemption comes to him from above and beyond human experience, it answers to his basic human need. Where Gilgamesh, Oedipus, and Lear fail, Christ succeeds, and the Christian succeeds with him as he recognizes that his human impasse as symbolized in Gilgamesh, Oedipus, and Lear is overcome by the love of God as incarnate in Christ.

When that fact is recognized in faith, the Christian is released from his impasse and his pilgrimage begins. No longer need he seek to purge his own guilt by the ceaseless masochism of imposing pain upon himself, or by the perpetual attempt to make a payment through good works whose very goodness is rendered futile by the motive of self-exaltation. The Christian in faith accepts the assurance that the pain has been borne and the service rendered so that he is released out of a bondage from which he could not escape. On his pilgrimage there is still suffering to be endured and work to be done, but the suffering and the service are no longer self-defeating. They are now caught up in the joy of an ultimate acceptance. Christopher Fry has described that acceptance and joy in his *Thor, With Angels:*

> I have seen our terrible gods come down
> To beg the crumbs which fall from our sins, their only
> Means of life. This evening you and I
> Can walk under the trees and be ourselves
> Together, knowing that this wild day has gone
> For good. . . .
>   I have heard
> Word of God, and felt our lonely flesh
> Welcome to creation. The fearful silence
> Became the silence of great sympathy,
> The quiet of God and man in the mutual word.
> And never again need we sacrifice, on and on
> And on, greedy of the gods' goodwill
> But always uncertain; for sacrifice
> Can only perfectly be made by God
> And sacrifice has so been made, by God
> To God in the body of God with man,
> On a tree set up at the four crossing roads
> Of earth, heaven, time and eternity
> Which meet upon that cross. . . .
> God give us courage to exist in God,
> And lonely flesh be welcome to creation.[1]

Appendix

Notes

Bibliography

Index

APPENDIX

PROTESTANTISM AND LITERARY STUDY

Martin Luther's statement, upon which this book opened, about the relation of literature to theology is quite significant for any analysis of the major Reformers' attitudes toward literature. Several points stand out in significance. In the first place, Luther here in effect gives his own answer to the question, which has so often been raised, as to whether the reformation would have been possible without the renaissance, and Luther's answer is that apart from the revival of learning (which, for the renaissance, was basically though of course not entirely literary learning) there would have been no reformation. He could not conceive, he said, of "a great revelation of the Word of God unless He had first prepared the way by the rise and prosperity of languages and letters, as though they were John the Baptists" and again he declares that there were no other means comparable to the study of poets and rhetoricians by which "people are wonderfully fitted for the grasping of sacred truth and for handling it skillfully and happily."[1] There can be no clearer statement than this one as to the importance of literary method for the study of Scripture, as Luther indicates his conviction that under God's providence the revival of literary study in the renaissance paved the way for the reformation of religion. In the second place, Luther also clearly indicates that literary study would continue to form the basis for a genuine understanding of Christianity. It was to literature, rather than to philosophy, that he turned as an ally, and he wrote that "without knowledge of literature pure theology cannot at all endure."[2] Philip Melanchthon spoke to precisely the same effect when he declared: "That religion be rightly taught . . . implies as a necessary condition sound instruction in Letters," and Laurence Chaderton, the great Puritan head of Emmanuel College, Cambridge, declared of rhetoric that

171

it "teacheth truly to discern proper speeches from those that are tropical and figurative."[3]

Few of us today are aware of the extent to which education in the sixteenth and seventeenth centuries was dominated by the Greek and Latin classics. Modern academic treatment of the sciences, social sciences, and modern literature had not been introduced at the time of the Reformation, and did not enter British education in any marked way until the time of the Puritan or Dissenting academies. In the meanwhile, beyond the most elementary introduction to alphabet and reading, education concentrated on classical language and classical writing, from the grammar schools (and the grammar studied was not English but Latin) through the universities.

One reason for the importance to Luther of the great languages of antiquity was that they were "the scabbard in which the Word of God is sheathed,"[4] but beyond this utilitarian recognition was his conviction of the benefit of literature in providing vicarious experience. It was generally agreed that by the study of literature insight was gained into human life, and that it was gained without the hazards of personal experiment. One learned from literary works as from laboratories of human experience. One of the educational leaders of Protestant England under Elizabeth I, Roger Ascham, wrote that "learning teacheth more in one year than experience in twenty, and learning teacheth safely, where experience maketh more miserable than wise."[5] Luther held the same general conviction, and expressed regret in his later life that he had not devoted more attention to the study of history and poetry. Karl Holl explains Luther's attitude as due to recognizing "the enrichment of the knowledge of life which he had thus lost. 'Much time is required for personal experience.' One shortens his course and avoids many errors when he learns from authors, and that means from history. For this reason, despite objectionable matter contained in them, he did not wish to omit even the comic poets, Terence and Plautus, in school because in them real life and real people are so excellently portrayed."[6]

And let us be very careful, here and elsewhere, not to draw too sharp a distinction between renaissance man and Christian man for, with relatively few exceptions, the two were in reality one man. Too frequently modern theologians of every Christian tradition have attacked the Renaissance in terms of misunderstandings and well-meaning misrepresentations which have oversimplified and falsified the true situation, as Prof. Herbert Weisinger has shown in his fine study, "The Attack on the Renaissance in Theology Today."[7] We can scarcely do better than to keep in mind Douglas Bush's classic definition: "Humanism in the Renaissance normally means Christian faith in alliance with God-given reason, which is the most human faculty in man. Humanism is that way of life and thought which keeps man in union with God and above the biological level."[8] Nor should we be too eager to make antitheses between Roman Catholic and Reformed attitudes toward classical studies. Father Edward Surtz has summarized Saint Thomas More's attitude toward classical learning in words which could be applied equally well to the leaders of the Protestant Reformation: "The function of even profane learning at a university . . . is to prepare the soul for an advanced and enlightened virtue. In addition, at the university a man should acquire prudence in dealing with human affairs, without which . . . even the theologian will shout nonsense to the ordinary people in his congregation."[9] Denominational lines do not mean much at this point, and if there was any difference it was that Protestants might have been more aware that man's sin kept him from putting fully into practice the good which he knew: "Our erected wit maketh us know what perfection is," as Sir Philip Sidney put it, "and yet our infected will keepeth us from reaching unto it."[10] But although natural depravity may not be overcome by education, still "delightful teaching" may temper man's evil and entice him to a larger measure of good. So the devout Reformed Churchman Sidney, while recognizing that the disease of the "infected will" can only finally be cured by divine grace, still praises the efficacy of humane literature which doth "imitate both to delight and teach; and delight to move men to take that goodness in hand, which without delight they would fly as from a stranger; and teach, to make them know that goodness whereunto they are moved: which being the noblest scope to which ever any learning was directed."[11]

Such was the underlying assumption of all the major Protestant efforts in education. Sturm, whose Protestant gymnasium at Strassburg became the model "of all the secondary schools of Europe,"[12] in his motto *Sapiens atque eloquens pietas* summarized the faith of the new learning that literary culture and wisdom would go hand in hand with piety. Sturm's purpose was to train "pious, learned, and eloquent men" for service in church and state, and in that double objective of service to church and commonwealth we see typified the movement to which he belonged. Martin Bucer similarly wished to develop effective citizens and good churchmen,[13] while Melanchthon declared that children should be "trained up to teach sound doctrine in the church, and to serve the state in a wise and able manner."[14] Beza, in his address to the first students at the newly inaugurated Geneva Academy, advised them that by serious instruction in true religion and the knowledge of *"bonnes lettres"* they could develop capacity to contribute to God's glory, to the support of their kindred, and the honor of their native land.[15] As early as 1538, study in Geneva was soundly based in the full range of the liberal arts: not only in the faith, but in the *"sciences humaines."*[16] As for the Academy itself, Quirinus Breen writes that "the leading idea of Calvin's Genevan Academy is that the new educational aim for students is to get a solid grounding in the arts and letters before they enter the professions. Even though you would be a preacher, be first a humanist, expresses his thought on the matter."[17]

It is not difficult to establish the fact that in Geneva the educational foundation was in the classics, and that theological studies came as a superstructure erected upon the classical foundation. The entire curriculum pursued prior to the professional study of theology was classical,[18] for Calvin believed that common grace could exist apart from saving grace and wrote that "the experience of all ages teacheth, how that as touching the furniture of this present life, the beams of God's glory hath always shined in unbelieving nations."[19] When Beza arrived in Geneva to be rector of the Academy, his first act was to open a course of lectures devoted to interpreting the orations of Demosthenes and certain books of Aristotle, to which he added readings from the

Holy Scriptures; and the duties of François Berauld, when he arrived as professor of Greek, were to offer a three-hour course of lectures in the form of commentary on Aristotle, Plato, *"Plutarque ou de quelque auteur crétien,"* and five hours of interpretation of the poets, orators, or historians.[20] Beza, in addressing the students of the Academy, reminded them that in pursuing their liberal arts education they were soldiers in the service of God and would one day render an account to their *"chef suprême"* of their performance in the holy mission of learning.[21]

In all these regards Geneva was typical of Protestant educational institutions; both Strassburg which preceded it and Edinburgh which stemmed from it followed similar courses. The reorganized Scottish university programs incorporated the classical curriculum of renaissance learning under Buchanan and the Melvilles, while at Melanchthon's Wittenberg "the subjects of university study were without exception reorganized on humanist principles with a thoroughness that would have satisfied Lorenzo Valla himself."[22] As far away as Lutheran Denmark the pattern was the same, and the leading educator there, Christian Pedersen, referred to a broad liberal arts curriculum in a typical fashion: "All these arts are none other than youth's delight and pleasure, when young people are properly taught them in their youth—studies which the Greeks in olden time taught their children."[23]

No one who has even the slightest acquaintance with the Reformers would suspect them of having regarded the study of classical writers as in any sense "saving." The grace of God alone could provide salvation, but humane learning could provide amelioration of the human condition, both for man individually and for society. Salvation is infinitely more valuable than amelioration, but the fact of salvation does not permit the Christian to omit any effort for personal and social amelioration. Indeed, it makes such effort a part of his service to God and to his neighbor. Effectual grace, which is the grace of salvation, is not the only work of God's spirit, for as Calvin put it the Holy Spirit "doth . . . nevertheless fill, move, and quicken all things with the virtue of the same spirit, and that according to the property

of every kind which he hath given to it by the law of creation."
God's good gifts operate among and through heathen and even
evil men, and if we neglect "the gifts of God, willingly offered in
them, we suffer just punishment for our slothfulness."[24]

For the Reformers, emphasis on literary learning meant almost
exclusively an emphasis on classical literature, since the vernacular European literatures had not yet been accepted as being on
a par with the works of Greece and Rome, and most modern subjects had not attained academic acceptance. As Woodward says
in his history of renaissance education, "Neither mathematics,
nor, in still greater degree, natural studies had attained organic
scientific exposition such as might render simplification for purposes of instruction possible to the teacher of the young."[25]
Bodies of knowledge must be systematized to the point where
they may be taught, and, to quote again from Woodward, "Before the seventeenth century no appropriate body of knowledge
existed except that embraced within the field of classical antiquity."[26] So the Reformers espoused classical education.

This system did not, of course, continue without challenge,
both implicit and explicit. Bacon, Comenius, Milton, and others
made the challenge explicit, but it was inherently presented in
the work of Copernicus, Galileo, Harvey, and others in science,
while in the field of literature which was so long the unchallenged
possession of Greek and Latin, giants arose within the vernacular
who made it increasingly difficult to justify a purely classical
training. The Puritan John Hall epitomized the newly developed
situation in which a purely classical education appeared anoma-
lous when he wrote, in an appeal to the Commonwealth Parlia-
ment for educational reform, that "he is not acquainted with the
business of knowledge, that knows not what sensible increases
(I had almost said perfections) it hath of late arrived to."[27]

During the Puritan Commonwealth period, repeated suggestions were put forward for the reform of education, and some attempts were made to the same end, but with the restoration of the
monarchy, according to R. F. Jones, educational reform was too
tainted with its Puritan associations to have much prospect of
success in the universities under a decidedly anti-Puritan regime.

Indeed, according to Jones, the reaction against the Puritans contributed greatly to the solidification of the traditional classical training in the English universities and Sir Eric Ashby, viewing the developments from a somewhat different angle, agrees.[28] That a period of stagnation set in for the two English universities, virtually all competent observers at the time, and scholars since, have agreed.

The conclusion of the Puritan interregnum with the restoration of the Stuart dynasty to the English throne and the re-establishment of Episcopacy brought many changes. The major changes in education, however, were indirectly produced, and stemmed from the fact that those who continued in their Puritan affirmations were excluded from the established English educational system. As a result, they had to chart a new course in education. Tragic though this circumstance must have seemed at the time, in the long range it proved quite heuristic. Freed from those traditional practices which, however necessary they may be for the preservation of an institution, also inhibit it from change, the English Dissenters were able to start afresh. Few educators have had so striking an opportunity as this which fell, unwanted, to the lot of the Dissenters. Many of Puritanism's most valuable developments came out of misfortunes which befell the movement, as with the development by Milton and others of a doctrine of free speech on the basis of irreconcilable conflicts of opinion. So with education, where after 1660 the Puritans (now Dissenters) were forced to start afresh. "As they were outside the pale of the older tradition and system," Jarman declares, "the Nonconformists were more open to new ideas and the modern subjects found a welcome in their schools."[29]

The influential developments within the Dissenting Academies have been recognized by many writers on education, but the subject was definitely treated only in 1954 by J. W. Ashley Smith in his meticulous study of the actual Academies, their curricular programs and assigned studies, their masters and the educational background and opinions of these masters.[30] No one who has even a cursory knowledge of English Dissent would expect that Smith would discover unanimity of practice prevalent throughout the Academies, and of course he has not done so. He has, however, discovered some remarkable patterns in the Academies, patterns which can only be regarded as significant. It was in the Academies—combining as they did secondary and university instruction—that certain major innovations were first employed on a wide scale. Here the study of English language and literature became a staple element in the curriculum. Well before 1700, John Woodhouse and Charles Morton required English written and oral composition and later Academies continued their pioneering work in the serious study of English composition and style.[31] Statutory instruction in English literature was also pioneered in the Academies, and Shakespeare evidently first became required reading for students in the Dissenting Academies, along with Spenser, Marlowe, Milton, Dryden, Butler, Pope, Addison, Sterne, Gray, and others. The Dissenting schoolmaster Enfield declared that "while science enriches the understanding, the study of polite literature cultivates the taste, and improves the heart, and both unite, to form the Accomplished and Happy Man."[32] Henry Grove, of Taunton Academy, declared that "tho' he allow'd Homer the praise of a very great genius" nonetheless "for beauty, variety, and grandeur of descriptions, as well as the true sublime in sentiments, he thought our countryman Milton infinitely preferable."[33] The canons of taste determining the Academies' selection of modern English authors appear, in so far as I can determine, to have been excellent, and both taste and boldness were required in the early eighteenth century to initiate the academic study of "moderns" such as *The Spectator* and *The Tatler* within a dozen years of their first appearance, as John Jennings did at Kibworth.[34] In addition to English, French language and literature were studied, including Fénelon's *Dialogues on Eloquence,* and the works of Racine, Corneille, and Pascal.[35]

It would be tempting to develop at length the other great contributions to modern education which were produced by the Dissenting Academies, innovations which laid the basis for modern instruction in history, the social sciences, and laboratory experimentation in natural science, but to do so would take us far afield from our primary concern with literature. The important point, for our purposes, is that the Puritans pioneered in the study of English literature, and were largely responsible for the study in schools and colleges of Shakespeare, Milton, and indeed the whole broad range of vernacular writing.

And that fact, taken in conjunction with the emphasis placed by the sixteenth-century reformation upon classical literature, completes in brief the evidence for the great emphasis placed upon literary learning during the first centuries of Protestantism. Much attention has been devoted to the relations between Protestantism and the rise of modern science. Of at least equal importance were the relations, which I have briefly traced, between literature and the early Protestant vitality. These are relations which contemporary Christians can neglect only to their own great loss.

NOTES

INTRODUCTION

1. Martin Luther, "Letter to Eoban Hess, March 29, 1523," *Luther's Correspondence,* trans. and ed. Preserved Smith and Charles M. Jacobs (United Lutheran Publication House, 1918), Vol. II, pp. 176–177.

2. Percy Bysshe Shelley, *A Defense of Poetry* in *The Prelude to Poetry: The English Poets in Defense and Praise of Their Own Art* (Everyman's Library, 1927), pp. 234, 241. Hereafter this anthology will be referred to as *The Prelude to Poetry.*

3. Charles G. Osgood, *Poetry as a Means of Grace* (Princeton University Press, 1946), p. 8.

CHAPTER ONE

1. Sir Philip Sidney, *An Apology for Poetry,* in *The Prelude to Poetry,* p. 44.

2. *Boccaccio on Poetry,* ed. Charles G. Osgood (Liberal Arts Press, Inc., 1956), pp. 47, 79.

3. Shelley, *A Defense of Poetry,* in *The Prelude to Poetry,* p. 239.

4. Richard R. Niebuhr, *Resurrection and Historical Reason* (Charles Scribner's Sons, 1957), p. 16.

5. Robert Sherwood, *Abe Lincoln in Illinois* (Charles Scribner's Sons, 1939), p. 190.

6. *Ibid.,* p. 189.

7. *Ibid.,* p. 197.

8. *Ibid.*

9. In the unpublished Candler Lectures delivered at Emory University in the fall of 1957.

10. George Bernard Shaw, *Saint Joan,* in *Selected Plays* (Dodd, Mead & Company, Inc., 1949), Vol. II, p. 314.

11. John Knox, *On the Meaning of Christ* (Charles Scribner's Sons, 1947), p. 80.

12. *Boccaccio on Poetry*, p. 49.

13. Sidney, *An Apology for Poetry*, in *The Prelude to Poetry*, p. 24.

14. Amos Wilder, "Scholars, Theologians, and Ancient Rhetoric," *Journal of Biblical Literature*, Vol. LXXV (1956), pp. 2, 6, 11.

15. Rudolf Bultmann, *Jesus Christ and Mythology* (Charles Scribner's Sons, 1958), p. 45.

16. Paul Elmer More, *The Religion of Plato* (Princeton University Press, 1921), pp. 14, 199, 205.

17. Rudolf Bultmann, *Myth and Christianity* (The Noonday Press, 1958), p. 70.

18. William Faulkner, *Faulkner at Nagano,* ed. Robert A. Jelliffe (Kenkyusha, Ltd., Publishers, Tokyo, 1956), p. 101. See also p. 206.

19. I regret to say that I have been unable to find the source of this quotation in Stevenson's works.

20. II Cor. 3:6. Unless otherwise indicated, all Biblical references are to the Authorized Version. Although the Revised Standard Version is a more accurate and intelligible translation, it remains true that the great literary influence of the Bible is from the Authorized Version, and for this reason it will be our standard source here.

21. J. Wolfgang Goethe, "Concerning Truth and the Appearance of Truth in Works of Art," *Seven Arts,* Vol. III, ed. Fernando Puma (Falcon's Wing Press, 1955), p. 221.

22. Ernest Short, *A History of Religious Architecture* (W. W. Norton & Company, Inc., n. d.), p. 39.

23. Edward A. Dowey, Jr., *The Knowledge of God in Calvin's Theology* (Columbia University Press, 1952), pp. 10, 3.

24. John Calvin, Commentary on Genesis 1:16, in *Calvin: Commentaries,* trans. and ed. Joseph Haroutunian (The Westminster Press, 1958), p. 356.

25. *Ibid.*

26. Amos Wilder, "Mythology and the New Testament: A

Review of *Kerygma and Mythos," Journal of Biblical Literature,*
Vol. LXIX (1950), p. 125.

27. Wilder, "Mythology and the New Testament," p. 124.

28. John Milton, *De Doctrina Christiana,* trans. Charles Sumner, *The Works of John Milton,* ed. Frank A. Patterson, *et al.*
(Columbia University Press, 1933), Vol. XIV, pp. 31, 33.

29. *Boccaccio on Poetry,* p. 63. See also pp. 48, 79.

30. John Calvin, *Calvin: Theological Treatises,* trans. J. K. S.
Reid (The Westminster Press, 1954), pp. 147, 101.

31. Bultmann, *Jesus Christ and Mythology,* pp. 36, 37.

32. *Ibid.,* p. 68.

33. Calvin, *Calvin: Theological Treatises,* p. 112.

34. John Milton, *Paradise Lost,* in *The Complete Poems and
Major Prose,* ed. Merritt Y. Hughes (Odyssey Press, Inc., 1957),
VIII, 113–114.

35. Bultmann, *Myth and Christianity,* p. 61. See also Bultmann, *Jesus Christ and Mythology,* p. 20.

36. Edwyn Bevan, *Symbolism and Belief* (George Allen & Unwin, Ltd., London, 1938), pp. 28–81, *passim.*

37. John Bunyan, *Pilgrim's Progress,* ed. J. B. Wharey (Clarendon Press, Oxford, 1928), p. 228.

38. Milton, *Paradise Lost,* X, 304–305.

39. Dante, *Paradiso,* XIX, 45, 49–51, in *The Portable Dante,*
trans. Laurence Binyon (The Viking Press, Inc., 1947). Unless
otherwise indicated, all references to the *Paradiso* are to the
Binyon edition.

40. *Ibid.,* I, 70–72.

41. Bunyan, *Pilgrim's Progress,* pp. 4–7, 181.

42. Milton, *Paradise Lost,* IV, 75, 16–23.

43. *Ibid.,* II, 650–653.

44. *Ibid.,* II, 795–802.

45. *Ibid.,* II, 744–745.

46. William Shakespeare, *Hamlet,* 3.1.56–60, in *The Complete
Works of Shakespeare,* ed. George L. Kittredge (Ginn & Company,
1936).

47. Leo Tolstoi, in *Writers on Writing,* ed. Walter Allen
(Phoenix House, Limited, London, 1948), p. 135.

48. Plato, *The Republic of Plato*, trans. J. L. Davies and D. J. Vaughan (Macmillan & Co., Ltd., London, 1935), 382D.

49. Benjamin Jowett, "Plato's Philosophy," in *The Works of Plato* (Dial Press, Inc., n. d.), Vol. I, p. lviii. Italics mine.

50. Luther, "Letter to Eoban Hess, March 29, 1523," *Luther's Correspondence*, Vol. II, pp. 176–177.

51. Bunyan, *Pilgrim's Progress*, p. 174.

CHAPTER TWO

1. Sidney, *An Apology for Poetry*, in *The Prelude to Poetry*, p. 16, and Robert Frost, from "The Figure a Poem Makes," in *Writers on Writing*, p. 22. The two anthologies from which these quotations are taken constitute excellent collections of the views expressed by literary men on the art of literature, and both will reward serious reading.

2. Frost, in *Writers on Writing*, p. 23.

3. Walt Whitman, Preface to *Leaves of Grass*, in *Writers on Writing*, p. 51.

4. Shaw, *Back to Methuselah*, in *Selected Plays*, Vol. II, p. 250.

5. Goethe, "World Literature," in *Seven Arts*, Vol. III, p. 225.

6. Faulkner, *Faulkner at Nagano*, pp. 95, 156, 177, 205.

7. Peter Abelard, quoted in Harbison's *The Christian Scholar in the Age of Reformation* (Charles Scribner's Sons, 1956), p. 37.

8. John Calvin, *Institutes of the Christian Religion*, trans. Thomas Norton (John Norton, London, 1611), II. ii. 15.

9. Faulkner, *op. cit.*, pp. 205, 35. See also p. 111.

10. C. S. Lewis, *The Abolition of Man* (The Macmillan Company, 1947), p. 12.

11. Calvin, *Institutes*, II. ii. 15.

12. Augustine, *City of God*, 15. 22.

13. Thomas Aquinas, *Summa Theologica* I–II, Q. 57, Art. 3.

14. Arnold Williams, *The Common Expositor: An Account of the Commentaries on Genesis, 1527–1633* (University of North Carolina Press, 1948), p. 145.

15. *Ibid.*, p. 146.

16. Quoted, without reference to source, in Edmund Fuller's

Man in Modern Fiction (Random House, Inc., 1958), p. 118.

17. Faulkner, *op. cit.*, p. 205.

18. *Ibid.*, pp. 13–14.

19. Gilbert Highet, "Mass Culture," a transcript of one of a series of radio talks printed and distributed by the Book-of-the-Month Club, 1957.

20. Martin Grotjahn, *Beyond Laughter* (McGraw-Hill Book Co., Inc., 1957), p. 153.

21. Alexander Pope, *Essay on Man*, II, 18, in *The Best of Pope*, ed. George Sherburn (Thomas Nelson & Sons, 1939).

22. Shelley, *A Defense of Poetry*, in *The Prelude to Poetry*, p. 216.

23. Shakespeare, *Hamlet*, 1. 1. 166–167.

24. Samuel Taylor Coleridge, *On the Principles of Genial Criticism Concerning the Fine Arts: Essay Third*, in *Biographia Literaria*, Vol. II, ed. J. Shawcross (Oxford University Press, London, 1954).

25. Christopher Fry, "Why Verse?" *World Theatre*, Vol. IV (1955), p. 59.

26. Coleridge, *op. cit.*, p. 239.

27. Aldous Huxley, *Brave New World Revisited* (Harper & Brothers, 1958), pp. 64–65.

28. Peter de Vries, *The Tunnel of Love* (Little, Brown & Co., 1954), pp. 11, 35, and *The Mackerel Plaza* (Little, Brown & Co., 1958), p. 36.

29. George Axelrod, *Will Success Spoil Rock Hunter?* (Bantam Books, Inc., 1957), p. 19.

30. Shakespeare, *Antony and Cleopatra*, 1. 2. 32.

31. *Ibid.*, 1. 2. 120–121.

32. *Ibid.*, 3. 4. 22–23.

33. *Ibid.*, 3. 7. 43 and 3. 10. 19.

34. *Ibid.*, 3. 13. 92–93.

35. *Ibid.*, 2. 2. 240–245.

36. *Ibid.*, 4. 1. 16 ff.

37. *Ibid.*, 5. 1. 30–31.

38. *Ibid.*, 1. 2. 133.

39. *Ibid.*, 3. 6. 66–67.

40. *Ibid.*, 4. 15. 18–21.

41. *Ibid.*, 4. 15. 33 and 5. 2. 193–194.

42. Shaw, *Saint Joan*, in *Selected Plays*, Vol. II, p. 295.

43. Huxley, *Brave New World* (Harper & Brothers, 1946), p. 254.

44. Leo Tolstoi, in *Seven Arts*, Vol. II, ed. Fernando Puma (Permabooks, 1954), p. 48.

45. Shelley, *The Defense of Poetry*, in *The Prelude to Poetry*, pp. 216–217.

46. Shakespeare, *King Lear*, 2. 4. 221–224.

47. *Ibid.*, 1. 4. 310–314.

48. *Ibid.*, 2. 4. 267–270.

49. Sophocles, *The Theban Plays*, trans. E. F. Watling (Penguin Books, Ltd., Harmondsworth, Middlesex, England, 1949), p. 143.

50. Euripides, *The Trojan Women*, trans. Edith Hamilton, in *The Greek Way to Western Civilization* (W. W. Norton & Company, Inc., 1930), p. 149. The translation which Miss Hamilton gives here differs from that in her *Three Greek Plays*, and seems to me more beautiful.

51. Shakespeare, *King Lear*, 4. 6. 109.

52. *Ibid.*, 3. 4. 28–36.

53. Euripides, *The Trojan Women*, in Hamilton, *The Greek Way*, p. 193.

54. Sophocles, *Antigone*, trans. Dudley Fitts and Robert Fitzgerald, in *Greek Plays in Modern Translation* (Dial Press, Inc., 1953), pp. 489, 497.

55. Euripides, *Hippolytus*, trans. Gilbert Murray, in *The Literature of Ancient Greece* (University of Chicago Press. Copyright, 1956, by the University of Chicago), p. 273.

56. Pope, *Essay on Man*, II, 8–10.

57. Pascal, *Pensées*, number 397.

58. Shakespeare, *King Lear*, 2. 4. 270.

CHAPTER THREE

1. Faulkner, *Faulkner at Nagano*, pp. 205, 206.

2. Alfred, Lord Tennyson, "Ulysses," lines 19–21.

3. Samuel Noah Kramer, *From the Tablets of Sumer* (Falcon's Wing Press, 1956), pp. 149–150.

4. Joseph Campbell, *The Hero with a Thousand Faces* (Pantheon Books, Inc., 1949), p. 367.

5. Bede, *Ecclesiastical History of the English Nation,* Book II, Ch. 13, in *Select Translations from Old English Prose,* ed. and trans. Albert S. Cook and Chauncey B. Tinker (Ginn & Company, 1908), p. 32.

6. Heb. 2:15.

7. Sophocles, *Oedipus at Colonus,* trans. Gilbert Murray, in *The Literature of Ancient Greece,* p. 249.

8. Horace, in *The Roman Way,* trans. Edith Hamilton (W. W. Norton & Company, Inc., 1932), p. 167.

9. Henri Frankfort *et al., The Intellectual Adventure of Ancient Man* (University of Chicago Press, 1946), p. 104, and *The Ruin,* trans. Charles W. Kennedy, in *Old English Elegies* (Princeton University Press, 1939), pp. 68–69.

10. Sophocles, *Antigone,* in *Greek Plays in Modern Translation,* p. 499.

11. Henry Wadsworth Longfellow, "Psalm of Life."

12. Shakespeare, *Macbeth,* 5. 5. 19–28.

13. Shakespeare, *Measure for Measure,* 3. 1. 118–132.

14. Psalms 8:5 and 49:12.

15. Shakespeare, *King Lear,* 3. 6. 81–82.

16. *Ibid.,* 1. 2. 1–2.

17. *Ibid.,* 1. 2. 11–12 and 5. 3. 174.

18. *Ibid.,* 3. 4. 52 ff.

19. *Ibid.,* 3. 4. 49–160, *passim.*

20. *Ibid.,* 3. 4. 111–112.

21. *Ibid.,* 1. 4. 250.

22. *Ibid.,* 4. 6. 97–108.

23. *Ibid.,* 4. 6. 136.

24. *Ibid.,* 4. 6. 109.

25. *Ibid.,* 4. 6. 210.

26. *Ibid.,* 5. 3. 190–199.

27. *Ibid.,* 5. 3. 313–315.

28. *Ibid.,* 5. 3. 318–319.

29. Pascal, *Pensées,* numbers 392, 397–398.

30. Thorkild Jacobsen, in Frankfort, *The Intellectual Adventure of Ancient Man,* p. 208.

31. *Ibid.,* pp. 209–210.

32. *Ibid.,* pp. 210–211.

33. *Beowulf,* trans. Charles W. Kennedy (Oxford University Press, 1940), lines 1551–1556, 1657–1661.

34. Sophocles, *The Theban Plays,* p. 59.

35. H. D. F. Kitto, *Greek Tragedy* (Doubleday Anchor Books, 1954), p. 145.

36. Sigmund Freud, "The Interpretation of Dreams," trans. A. A. Brill, in *The Basic Writings of Sigmund Freud* (Modern Library, Inc., 1938), p. 308.

37. Erich Fromm, *The Forgotten Language* (Holt, Rinehart and Winston, Inc., 1951), p. 201.

38. *Ibid.,* p. 218. See also second choral dialogue, *Oedipus at Colonus,* trans. Robert Fitzgerald, in *Greek Plays in Modern Translation,* pp. 406–407.

39. Kitto, *op. cit.,* p. 154.

40. Francis Fergusson, *The Idea of a Theatre* (Princeton University Press, 1949), p. 18.

41. Sophocles, *The Theban Plays,* p. 68.

42. *Ibid.,* p. 26.

43. *Ibid.*

44. *Ibid.,* pp. 29, 32.

45. Sophocles, *King Oedipus,* trans. W. B. Yeats, in *Greek Plays in Modern Translation,* p. 356.

46. Sophocles, *The Theban Plays,* pp. 55, 64.

47. *Ibid.,* p. 48.

48. Matthew Arnold, "Dover Beach," lines 15–18.

49. Sophocles, *The Theban Plays,* p. 55.

50. *Ibid.,* p. 63.

51. *Ibid.,* p. 62.

CHAPTER FOUR

1. Sophocles, *The Theban Plays,* p. 48.

2. *Ibid.,* p. 59.

3. Rom. 7:24.

4. Sophocles, *The Theban Plays*, p. 62.

5. Advent Lyrics from *Christ I*, trans. Charles W. Kennedy, *Early English Christian Poetry* (Hollis & Carter, Ltd., Publishers, London, 1952), pp. 85–87.

6. *Ibid.*, p. 87.

7. Christopher Fry, *A Sleep of Prisoners* (Oxford University Press, 1951), p. 42.

8. *Ibid.*, p. 43.

9. The passages involving the son of heaven and the three prisoners may all be found in Fry's *A Sleep of Prisoners*, pp. 44–48.

10. T. S. Eliot, *The Complete Poems and Plays* (Harcourt, Brace and Company, Inc., 1952), p. 56.

11. *Ibid.*, pp. 105–106.

12. *Ibid.*, p. 104.

13. *Ibid.*, p. 103.

14. T. S. Eliot, *The Cocktail Party* (Harcourt, Brace and Company, Inc., 1950), p. 142.

15. *Ibid.*, p. 98.

16. Heinrich Quistorp, *Calvin's Doctrine of the Last Things*, trans. Harold Knight (John Knox Press, 1955), p. 75.

17. T. S. Eliot, *Murder in the Cathedral* (Harcourt, Brace and Company, Inc., 1935), p. 70.

18. Sophocles, *The Theban Plays*, pp. 61, 63.

19. Christopher Fry, *The Lady's Not for Burning* (Oxford University Press, 1954), p. 57.

20. Shaw, *Major Barbara*, in *Selected Plays*, Vol. I, pp. 383, 394.

21. Eliot, *Murder in the Cathedral*, p. 16.

22. *Ibid.*, p. 44.

23. *Ibid.*, p. 40.

24. Milton, *Paradise Lost*, III, 290–294.

25. William Langland, *Piers Plowman*, ed. Henry W. Wells (Sheed & Ward, Ltd., 1938), Passus XVII.

26. Christopher Fry, *Thor, With Angels* (Oxford University Press, 1954), pp. 51–52.

27. D. M. Baillie, *God Was in Christ: An Essay on Incarnation and Atonement* (Charles Scribner's Sons, 1948), p. 171.

28. Aeschylus, *Prometheus Bound,* trans. Edith Hamilton, in *Greek Plays in Modern Translation,* p. 540.

29. *Ibid.,* p. 538.

30. II Cor. 5:18–19. The reference here is to the Revised Standard Version.

31. Milton, *Paradise Lost,* III, 205; V, 77–78; IX, 547. For a full analysis of these themes in *Paradise Lost,* see my *God, Man, and Satan: The Patterns of Christian Thought and Life in "Paradise Lost," "Pilgrim's Progress," and the Great Theologians* (Princeton University Press, 1960).

32. See R. N. Dandekar, "The Role of Man in Hinduism," in *The Religion of the Hindus,* ed. Kenneth W. Morgan (The Ronald Press Company, 1953), pp. 122, 125, 131.

33. Milton, *Paradise Lost,* IX, 710, 713–714.

34. *Ibid.,* IX, 866.

35. *Bṛhad-āraṇyaka Upaniṣad,* I, iv, 10, in *The Principal Upaniṣads,* ed. and trans. S. Radhakrishnan (Harper & Brothers, 1953), p. 168.

36. Milton, *Paradise Lost,* IX, 547.

37. *Ibid.,* X, 111–115.

38. *Ibid.,* IX, 1187–1189.

39. *Ibid.,* IX, 1121–1126.

40. *Ibid.,* VIII, 571–573.

41. *Ibid.,* IX, 1056–1058.

42. *Ibid.,* IV, 313–314.

43. *Ibid.,* IX, 858.

44. *Ibid.,* IV, 509–511.

45. *Ibid.,* X, 842–844.

46. *Ibid.,* X, 1006.

47. *Ibid.,* X, 1044–1045.

48. Augustine, *Augustine: Earlier Writings,* trans. and ed. John H. S. Burleigh (The Westminster Press, 1953), p. 260.

49. Milton, *Paradise Lost,* XII, 404–410.

50. Augustine, *De Doctrina Christiana,* trans. D. W. Robertson, Jr. (Liberal Arts Press, Inc., 1958), 3. 10. 16.

51. Fry, *Thor, With Angels,* pp. 28–29.

52. *Ibid.,* p. 29.

53. Milton, *Paradise Lost,* III, 252.

54. *Ibid.,* XII, 571.

55. *Ibid.,* X, 633–637.

56. *Ibid.,* XII, 469–473.

CHAPTER FIVE

1. Bunyan, *Pilgrim's Progress,* pp. 172, 238.

2. Milton, *Paradise Lost,* IV, 75, and X, 598.

3. *Ibid.,* IX, 467–468, and 122–123.

4. Bunyan, *Pilgrim's Progress,* pp. 173, 238, and 61–62.

5. *Ibid.,* p. 309.

6. *Ibid.,* pp. 249, 73.

7. Langland, *Piers Plowman,* V, 643.

8. *Ibid.,* V, 651–655.

9. *Ibid.,* V, 662.

10. *Ibid.,* V, 663–664.

11. *Ibid.,* V, 665–667.

12. *Ibid.,* V, 685–686.

13. *Ibid.,* VII, 217, 241–245, and V, 768 ff.

14. *Ibid.,* V, 743–746.

15. *Ibid.,* V, 747–755.

16. *Ibid.,* VI, 106.

17. *Ibid.,* VII, 243.

18. *Ibid.,* XX, 181.

19. *Ibid.,* XX, 356–358.

20. *Ibid.,* XX, 171.

21. *Ibid.,* XX, 365–369.

22. Milton, *Paradise Lost,* XII, 524–526.

23. Dante, *Paradiso,* XVIII, 122; XXII, 77; XVII, 51.

24. *Ibid.,* XXIX, 115–117.

25. Milton, *Lycidas,* lines 123–127.

26. Dante, *Paradiso,* XXVII, 22–27.

27. Carl Sandburg, "To a Contemporary Bunkshooter," in

Complete Poems (Harcourt, Brace and Company, Inc., 1950), pp. 29–30.

28. Eugene O'Neill, *The Hairy Ape* in *The Plays of Eugene O'Neill* (Charles Scribner's Sons, 1935), Vol. V, p. 218.

29. Shaw, *Major Barbara,* in *Selected Plays,* Vol. I, p. 329.

30. J. D. Salinger, *The Catcher in the Rye* (Little, Brown & Co., 1951), p. 178.

31. de Vries, *The Mackerel Plaza*, p. 4.

32. *Ibid.,* pp. 4, 7–8.

33. Tennessee Williams, *Cat on a Hot Tin Roof* (New Directions, 1955), p. 100.

34. Geddes MacGregor, *From a Christian Ghetto* (Longmans, Green & Co., Ltd., London, 1954), p. 26.

35. *Ibid.,* p. 93.

36. *Ibid.,* pp. 95–96.

37. *Ibid.,* pp. 98, 99, 100.

38. Bunyan, *Pilgrim's Progress,* pp. 309–310.

39. For a detailed analysis of this allegory, see my *God, Man, and Satan: The Patterns of Christian Thought and Life in "Paradise Lost," "Pilgrim's Progress," and the Great Theologians* (Princeton University Press, 1960).

40. Milton, *Samson Agonistes,* lines 529, 532, 80–82, 99–102.

41. *Ibid.,* 460–462.

42. *Ibid.,* 647.

43. *Ibid.,* 649–651.

44. *Ibid.,* 914–918.

45. *Ibid.,* 949–950.

46. Bunyan, *Pilgrim's Progress,* p. 62.

47. *Ibid.,* p. 63.

48. Milton, *Samson Agonistes,* lines 1168–1177.

49. *Ibid.,* 1719–1721.

50. *Ibid.,* 1381–1383.

51. *Ibid.,* 1511–1512.

52. *Ibid.,* 1745–1758.

53. Heb. 11:10.

54. Bunyan, *Pilgrim's Progress,* p. 326.

55. *Ibid.,* p. 325.

56. Dante, *Paradiso*, VII, 58–60.
57. *Ibid.*, XXX, 40–42.
58. *Ibid.*, XXXIII, 145, 54, and 86–87 in the Dent edition.
59. *Ibid.*, XXXIII, 140–141.
60. *Ibid.*, XXXIII, 142–145.

EPILOGUE

1. Fry, *Thor, With Angels,* pp. 51–52, 54.

APPENDIX:

PROTESTANTISM AND LITERARY STUDY

1. Martin Luther, "Letter to Eoban Hess, March 29, 1523," in *Luther's Correspondence*, Vol. II, 176–177.
2. *Ibid.*
3. William H. Woodward, *Studies in Education During the Age of the Renaissance: 1400–1600* (Cambridge University Press, Cambridge, 1906), p. 224, and Mark H. Curtis, *Oxford and Cambridge in Transition: 1558–1642* (Clarendon Press, Oxford, 1959), p. 206.
4. Martin Luther, "Letters to the Mayors and Aldermen," in *Luther on Education,* ed. F. V. N. Painter (Concordia Publishing House, 1928), p. 186.
5. Roger Ascham, *The Scholemaster,* ed. J. E. B. Mayor and Hartley Coleridge (G. Bell & Sons, Ltd., London, 1934), p. 113. Ascham here, like most Protestant humanists, is speaking of classical learning in terms virtually indistinguishable from those of Roman Catholic humanists, and indeed at this point is merely paraphrasing Erasmus' *De Pueris Instituendis,* ed. William H. Woodward in *Erasmus Concerning the Aim and Method of Education* (Cambridge University Press, Cambridge, 1904), pp. 191–192.

6. Karl Holl, *The Cultural Significance of the Reformation* (Meridian Books, Inc., 1959), p. 116, and *The Works of Martin Luther* (United Lutheran Publication House, 1931), Vol. IV, pp. 117, 123. Luther here takes the same position as that adopted by Erasmus relative to "immoral" situations as treated by the poets, and holds that poetry should be studied even so. Some Renaissance educators, both Protestant and Roman Catholic, differed from Luther and Erasmus on this issue and were highly skeptical of teaching certain pagan works, but such suspicions seem to spring from individual temperaments and not to follow denominational lines. Thus Cardinal Pole in 1556 sent injunctions to Oxford and Cambridge that lecturers in philosophy "should as far as possible follow the opinions of those who differed least from Christian truth" (Charles E. Mallet, *A History of the University of Oxford* [Longmans, Green & Co., Inc., 1924], Vol. II, p. 102), and Colet preferred the use of Christian Latin poets (Woodward, *Studies in Education,* p. 237) while in the regulations for the Elizabethan grammar school at Thame, we find the injunction that "if any passage or blemish occur in these [classical] authors . . . which may be injurious to true piety or good morals, it shall be passed over, as it were dryshod, without being touched" (J. Howard Brown, *Elizabethan Schooldays* [Basil Blackwell, Oxford, 1933], p. 74). It is, finally, interesting to note that both the Roman Catholic Vives (in *De Tradendis Disciplinis,* trans. Foster Watson as *Vives: On Education* [Cambridge University Press, Cambridge, 1913], p. 128) and the Protestant Comenius (Chapter XXV of *The Great Didactic*) recommend expurgation of objectionable matter in pagan authors.

7. Herbert Weisinger, "The Attack on the Renaissance in Theology Today," *Studies in the Renaissance,* Vol. II (1955), pp. 176–189.

8. Douglas Bush, *The Renaissance and English Humanism* (University of Toronto Press, Toronto, 1958), p. 54.

9. Edward Surtz, S. J., *The Praise of Pleasure: Philosophy, Education, and Communism in More's "Utopia"* (Harvard University Press, 1957), p. 127.

10. Sir Philip Sidney, *Apologie for Poetrie,* ed. Evelyn S.

Shuckburgh (Cambridge University Press, Cambridge, 1951), p. 9.

11. *Ibid.*, p. 11.

12. S. S. Laurie, *Studies in the History of Educational Opinion from the Renaissance* (Cambridge University Press, Cambridge, 1905), p. 26.

13. Hastings Eells, *Martin Bucer* (Yale University Press, 1931), p. 47.

14. Frederick Eby, *Early Protestant Educators* (McGraw-Hill Book Co., Inc., 1931), p. 180.

15. Charles Borgeaud, *Histoire de l'Université de Geneve* (Geneva, 1900), pp. 48–49.

16. *Ibid.*, p. 17.

17. Quirinus Breen, *John Calvin: A Study in French Humanism* (Wm. B. Eerdmans Publishing Company, 1931), pp. 154–155.

18. Borgeaud, *op. cit.*, pp. 43–44.

19. Quoted from Calvin's *Commentary on Genesis* in Arnold Williams, *The Common Expositor,* pp. 145–146.

20. Borgeaud, *op. cit.*, pp. 40 and 66.

21. *Ibid.*, p. 49.

22. M. L. Clarke, *Classical Education in Britain: 1500–1900* (Cambridge University Press, Cambridge, 1959), pp. 140–142, and Woodward, *Studies in Education,* p. 230.

23. E. H. Dunkley, *The Reformation in Denmark* (S.P.C.K., London, 1948), p. 108.

24. John Calvin, *Institutes of the Christian Religion,* trans. John Norton, II. ii. 16.

25. Woodward, *Studies in Education,* p. 241.

26. *Ibid.*, p. 243.

27. Richard F. Jones, *Ancients and Moderns* (Washington University Studies, 1936), p. 101.

28. *Ibid.*, pp. 181, 280–282, and Sir Eric Ashby, *Technology and the Academics* (Macmillan & Co., Ltd., London, 1959), p. 6.

29. T. L. Jarman, *Landmarks in the History of Education* (Philosophical Library, Inc., 1952), p. 190.

30. J. W. Ashley Smith, *The Birth of Modern Education: The Contributions of the Dissenting Academies 1660–1800* (Independent Press, Ltd., London, 1954).

31. *Ibid.*, p. 238.
32. *Ibid.*, p. 166.
33. *Ibid.*, pp. 100–101.
34. *Ibid.*, p. 112.
35. *Ibid.*, pp. 114 and 222.

BIBLIOGRAPHY
PRINCIPAL WORKS CITED

Aeschylus, *Prometheus Bound*, trans. Edith Hamilton, in *Greek Plays in Modern Translation*. Dial Press, Inc., 1947.

Aquinas, Thomas, *Summa Theologica*, in *Introduction to St. Thomas Aquinas*, ed. Anton C. Pegis. Random House, Inc., 1948.

Augustine, *The Basic Writings of Saint Augustine*, 2 vols., ed. Whitney J. Oates. Random House, Inc., 1948.

——— *De Doctrina Christiana*, trans. D. W. Robertson, Jr. Liberal Arts Press, Inc., 1958.

——— *Augustine: Earlier Writings*, trans. and ed. John H. S. Burleigh. The Westminster Press, 1953.

Axelrod, George, *Will Success Spoil Rock Hunter?* Bantam Books, Inc., 1957.

Baillie, D. M., *God Was in Christ: An Essay on Incarnation and Atonement.* Charles Scribner's Sons, 1948.

Bede, *Ecclesiastical History of the English Nation*, in *Select Translations from Old English Prose*, ed. and trans. Albert S. Cook and Chauncey B. Tinker. Ginn & Company, 1908.

Beowulf, trans. Charles W. Kennedy. Oxford University Press, 1940.

Bevan, Edwyn, *Symbolism and Belief*. George Allen & Unwin, Ltd., London, 1938.

Boccaccio on Poetry, ed. Charles G. Osgood. Liberal Arts Press, Inc., 1956.

Bultmann, Rudolf, *Jesus Christ and Mythology*. Charles Scribner's Sons, 1958.

——— *Myth and Christianity*. The Noonday Press, 1958.

Bunyan, John, *Pilgrim's Progress*, ed. J. B. Wharey. Clarendon Press, Oxford, 1928.

Calvin, John, *Calvin: Commentaries*, trans. and ed. Joseph Haroutunian. The Westminster Press, 1958.

———— *Institutes of the Christian Religion,* trans. Thomas Norton. John Norton, London, 1611.

———— *Calvin: Theological Treatises,* trans. J. K. S. Reid. The Westminster Press, 1954.

Campbell, Joseph, *The Hero with a Thousand Faces.* Pantheon Books, Inc., 1949.

Coleridge, Samuel Taylor, *Biographia Literaria,* 2 vols., ed. J. Shawcross. Oxford University Press, London, 1954.

Dandekar, R. N., "The Role of Man in Hinduism," in *The Religion of the Hindus,* ed. Kenneth W. Morgan. The Ronald Press Company, 1953.

Dante, *Dante's Paradiso,* ed. Rev. Philip H. Wicksteed and H. Oelsner. J. M. Dent & Sons, Ltd., Publishers, Edinburgh, 1946.

———— *The Portable Dante,* trans. Laurence Binyon. The Viking Press, Inc., 1947.

de Vries, Peter, *The Mackerel Plaza.* Little, Brown & Co., 1958.

———— *The Tunnel of Love.* Little, Brown & Co., 1954.

Dowey, Edward A., Jr., *The Knowledge of God in Calvin's Theology.* Columbia University Press, 1952.

Eliot, T. S., *The Cocktail Party.* Harcourt, Brace and Company, Inc., 1950.

———— *The Complete Poems and Plays.* Harcourt, Brace and Company, Inc., 1952.

———— *Murder in the Cathedral.* Harcourt, Brace and Company, Inc., 1935.

Faulkner, William, *Faulkner at Nagano.* Kenkyusha, Ltd., Publishers, Tokyo, 1956.

Fergusson, Francis, *The Idea of a Theatre.* Princeton University Press, 1949.

Frankfort, Henri, *et al.,* *The Intellectual Adventure of Ancient Man.* University of Chicago Press, 1946.

Freud, Sigmund, "The Interpretation of Dreams," trans. A. A. Brill, in *The Basic Writings of Sigmund Freud.* Modern Library, Inc., 1938.

Fromm, Erich, *The Forgotten Language.* Holt, Rinehart and Winston, Inc., 1951.

Fry, Christopher, *The Lady's Not for Burning.* Oxford University Press, 1954.

————— *A Sleep of Prisoners*. Oxford University Press, 1951.

————— *Thor, With Angels*. Oxford University Press, 1954.

Fuller, Edmund, *Man in Modern Fiction*. Random House, Inc., 1958.

Goethe, J. Wolfgang, "Concerning Truth and the Appearance of Truth in Works of Art," *Seven Arts,* Vol. III, ed. Fernando Puma. Falcon's Wing Press, 1955.

Greek Plays in Modern Translation, ed. Dudley Fitts. Dial Press, Inc., 1953.

Grotjahn, Martin, *Beyond Laughter*. McGraw-Hill Book Co., Inc., 1957.

Hamilton, Edith, *The Greek Way to Western Civilization*. W. W. Norton & Company, Inc., 1930.

————— *The Roman Way*. W. W. Norton & Company, Inc., 1932.

Harbison, E. Harris, *The Christian Scholar in the Age of Reformation*. Charles Scribner's Sons, 1956.

Highet, Gilbert, "Mass Culture." Book-of-the-Month Club, 1957.

Huxley, Aldous, *Brave New World*. Harper & Brothers, 1946.

————— *Brave New World Revisited*. Harper & Brothers, 1958.

Kennedy, Charles W., trans., *Beowulf*. Oxford University Press, 1940.

————— trans., *Early English Christian Poetry*. Hollis & Carter, Ltd., Publishers, London, 1952.

————— trans., *Old English Elegies*. Princeton University Press, 1939.

Kitto, H. D. F., *Greek Tragedy*. Doubleday Anchor Books, 1954.

Knox, John, *On the Meaning of Christ*. Charles Scribner's Sons, 1947.

Kramer, Samuel Noah, *From the Tablets of Sumer*. Falcon's Wing Press, 1956.

Langland, William, *Piers Plowman,* ed. Henry W. Wells. Sheed & Ward, Ltd., London, 1938.

Lewis, C. S., *The Abolition of Man*. The Macmillan Company, 1947.

Luther, Martin, *Luther's Correspondence,* trans. and ed. Preserved Smith and Charles M. Jacobs. United Lutheran Publication House, 1918.

MacGregor, Geddes, *From a Christian Ghetto*. Longmans, Green & Co., Ltd., London, 1954.

Milton, John, *The Complete Poems and Major Prose*, ed. Merritt Y. Hughes. Odyssey Press, Inc., 1957.

——— *De Doctrina Christiana*, trans. Charles Sumner, in *The Works of John Milton*, ed. Frank A. Patterson, *et al.*, Vol. XIV. Columbia University Press, 1933.

More, Paul Elmer, *The Religion of Plato*. Princeton University Press, 1921.

Murray, Gilbert, *The Literature of Ancient Greece*. University of Chicago Press, 1956.

Niebuhr, Richard R., *Resurrection and Historical Reason*. Charles Scribner's Sons, 1957.

O'Neill, Eugene, *The Hairy Ape* in *The Plays of Eugene O'Neill*. Charles Scribner's Sons, 1935.

Osgood, Charles G., *Poetry as a Means of Grace*. Princeton University Press, 1946.

Pascal, Blaise, *Pensées and the Provincial Letters*, trans. W. F. Trotter and Thomas McCrie. Random House, Inc., 1941.

Plato, *The Republic of Plato*, trans. J. L. Davies and D. J. Vaughan. Macmillan & Co., Ltd., London, 1935.

——— *The Works of Plato*, trans. B. Jowett, 4 vols. Dial Press, Inc., n. d.

Pope, Alexander, *Essay on Man* in *The Best of Pope*, ed. George Sherburn. Thomas Nelson & Sons, 1939.

The Prelude to Poetry: The English Poets in Defense and Praise of Their Own Art. Everyman's Library, London and New York, 1927.

The Principal Upaniṣads, ed. and trans. S. Radhakrishnan. Harper & Brothers, 1953.

Quistorp, Heinrich, *Calvin's Doctrine of the Last Things*, trans. Harold Knight. John Knox Press, 1955.

Salinger, J. D., *The Catcher in the Rye*. Little, Brown & Co., 1951.

Sandburg, Carl, *Complete Poems*. Harcourt, Brace and Company, Inc., 1950.

Seven Arts, Vol. II, ed. Fernando Puma. Permabooks, 1954.

Seven Arts, Vol. III, ed. Fernando Puma. Falcon's Wing Press, 1955.

Shakespeare, William, *The Complete Works of Shakespeare,* ed. George L. Kittredge. Ginn & Company, 1936.

Shaw, George Bernard, *Selected Plays,* 4 vols. Dodd, Mead & Company, Inc., 1949.

Shelley, Percy Bysshe, *A Defense of Poetry,* in *The Prelude to Poetry.*

Sherwood, Robert, *Abe Lincoln in Illinois.* Charles Scribner's Sons, 1939.

Short, Ernest, *A History of Religious Architecture.* W. W. Norton & Company, Inc., n. d.

Sidney, Sir Philip, *An Apology for Poetry,* in *The Prelude to Poetry.*

Sophocles, *Antigone,* trans. Dudley Fitts and Robert Fitzgerald, in *Greek Plays in Modern Translation.* Dial Press, Inc., 1953.

———— *The Theban Plays,* trans. E. F. Watling. Penguin Books, Ltd., Harmondsworth, Middlesex, England, 1949.

Taylor, A. E., *Socrates.* Doubleday Anchor Books, 1956.

Wilder, Amos, "Mythology and the New Testament: A Review of *Kerygma and Mythos,*" *Journal of Biblical Literature,* Vol. LXIX (1950), pp. 113–127.

———— "Scholars, Theologians, and Ancient Rhetoric," *Journal of Biblical Literature,* Vol. LXXV (1956), pp. 1–11.

Williams, Arnold, *The Common Expositor: An Account of the Commentaries on Genesis, 1527–1633.* University of North Carolina Press, 1948.

Williams, Tennessee, *Cat on a Hot Tin Roof.* New Directions, 1955.

Writers on Writing, ed. Walter Allen. Phoenix House, Limited, London, 1948.

INDEX

Virgil, 59

Weisinger, Herbert, 173
Whitman, Walt, 58
Wilder, Amos, 40
Williams, Charles, 62
Williams, Tennessee, 148

*Will   Success   Spoil   Rock
    Hunter?* 69
Woodhouse, John, 178
Woodward, W. H., 176

Zwingli, Ulrich, 14